THE TOWERS OF DUNVEGAN

Autumns in Skye Ross and Sutherland

T. RATCLIFFE BARNETT

WITH 16 ILLUSTRATIONS

EDINBURGH

ROBERT GRANT & SON

126 PRINCES STREET

1930

Printed in Great Britain
by Turnbull & Spears, Edinburgh

ISLE OF MY HEART

SKYE OF THE COOLINS

TO THE MEMORY OF THAT GREAT SKYEMAN——SHERIFF NICOLSON

Down the long winding streets of romance
    Walk I enchanted,
Where all my heart-strings of love are twined
    Round each tall dwelling,
And the sea haar is kissed by the warm
    Sunlight from heaven.

Oft do I brood on the high rock shrine,
    Lost in old mem'ries ;
Seeing the clansmen stript for the fight
    With foreign foemen ;
Hearing the sennachies proudly sing
    Scotland's brave story.

But, when the west wind blows from the hills
    Over the lowlands,
And all the fields are braided with green,
    Firstfruits of harvest,
Then, O my heart, I hear the call
    Of the dear islands ;

And of that road which stretches far north
    Over the moorlands,
Where the blue mountains, like sentries, stand
    Guarding the green glens ;
Land of brave heroes long since sleeping
    After their battles.

There, buoyed above the restless sea waves,
    Brown sails all flapping,
Riding in sunlight the birlinn waits
    To take me over ;
Fresh breezes whispering songs of love
    Through rope and rattling.

Over to Skye, the Isle of my Heart,
    Where in the old years
When youth and glamour glowed on my brow
    I found great wonders.
Splintered mountains in splendour rising
    Into the heavens ;

Sea lochs crowded with Viking stories,
    And castles hoary ;
Green straths dotted with old black houses,
    Where dwelt fine seamen ;
Peat reek rising like evening incense
    From homely altars.

Round each grey castle Ossian's giants
    Had great encounters ;
Bragela, queen of the Misty Isle,
    And mighty Cuchullin ;
Epics of battle, idylls of love,
    Still told in ceilidh.

Gone are the chieftains, ruined their halls,
    Centuries old now ;
Stark walls on headlands washed by the rain
    Gleam in the sunbursts ;
Wind from the Coolins sighing laments
    Over the lost days.

Oft in my wakeful hours do I dream
    Of thy wild mountains
Rising like blue clouds out of the sea
    In summer sunshine ;
Hearing the lilt of soft Gaelic tongues
    Bidding me welcome.

Yours be the love, O Skye, that outlives
    All generations ;
Burning, like peat fires that never die,
    For thy dear people ;
Home of my Heart and Isle of my Dreams,
    Skye of the Coolins.

EDINBURGH, *May* 1930

FOREWORD

THOMAS DE QUINCEY—that celestial tramp—in his
"Confessions of an English Opium-Eater," com-
ments on the justness of a remark of Dr Johnson,
that "we never do anything for the last time (of
things, that is, which we have long been in the
habit of doing) without sadness of heart."

Having now reached the farthest bounds of
Scotland, I must confess to a certain feeling of
regret that this is the last of a series of four travel
books on the Lowlands and Highlands which have
given me much pleasure to write. Almost all the
articles have appeared in *The Scotsman*; one or
two are reprinted from the *S.M.T. Magazine*;
and that on "The Ten Commandments of Walking" was given as a wireless talk. For permission
to reprint them, I am indebted to the editors of
these journals, and to the British Broadcasting
Corporation. All the photographs have been
supplied by that genial friend of mountaineers,
Mr George Sang, W.S., the secretary of the Scottish
Mountaineering Club, whose never-failing kindness
I here most gratefully acknowledge.

In every book of travel there must of necessity
be a large number of historic statements, and there
is nothing easier than making a slip. But, having
done my best to verify every statement, I now
gladly acknowledge the countless authorities to

7

which I am indebted, and also the various poets quoted, without whose golden words some of the chapters would have lost their richest touch.

So long as there are roads in this beloved land, each generation will set out anew to discover traveller's joy. To one and all who seek the unspeakable pleasures which I myself have tasted, I can only say—May Good Luck attend you.

T. R. B.

CONTENTS

SKYE

ROSS

SUTHERLAND

LIST OF ILLUSTRATIONS

SKYE

ROSS

SUTHERLAND

AUTUMNS IN SKYE

I

SKYE

THE ISLAND OF MY HEART

I NEVER think of the Isle of Skye but I am reminded of three great English writers who, one after the other, determined to write an adequate appreciation of that superb Hebrew drama—the Book of Job. The wonder of it so oppressed them that they never could make a beginning. So they all died without having put pen to paper.

And yet ! the Isle of Mist is so compelling, that the veriest scribbler keeps writing love notes on it every time he thinks of the heavenly days and magic nights he has spent in that paradise of the West.

In winter time, when the fog rolls along the city streets, and all the beauties of the world are blotted out in gloom, the Skye-lover will plough his way through the crowd with a far-ben look on his face and lips that keep muttering some soundless rune. At that moment he is seeing the distant Coolins, blue and ethereal. The summer sun is blazing down on the purple heather at his feet, and the warm air is drugged with the scent of honey and bog-myrtle. Instead of the roar of city traffic he hears the crash of great seas on the mighty headlands of Bracadale, or the wind roaring in the shrouds of the old boat as she thrashes her way between Hunish Head and Trodday Isle, her dripping bows pointing bravely across the Minch for the Outer Isles.

It was this undying hunger in the heart that made Alexander Nicolson write—

> My heart is yearning for thee, O Skye,
> Dearest of islands.

It is this same compulsion of love that makes it as inevitable for the wandering man to unburden himself about Skye, as for the lover to be for ever sending passionate epistles to the mistress of his heart.

Skye! The Isle of Mist. The Winged Isle. Eilean a Cheo. Eilean Sgitheanach—the Island of Skyants or Skye Folks. Call it what you will, the very name has something mystical about it, something of that high geste which fills the soul with dreams of Ossian's heroes, and brings you very near the island rovers who lived of old in yon stark castles which turn their eyeless windows to the grumbling seas.

There are many ways of approaching Skye. You may travel all the way from London to Kyle in a touring car, and cross the narrow strait in an open ferry-boat, your luxurious glass coach perched precariously on two planks placed athwart the gunwales. Then, when you scramble out on the stone pier at Kyleakin, you will be standing on the very doorstep of Skye. But, although that is a glamorous road to Skye, yet it is not the best.

CLIFFS AT TALISKER BAY

I like to remember that I saw Skye first from the white deck of a schooner as we raced northwards from Mull on a blue day in June. Those were the days long before auxiliary screws or motor-cars. From a bundle of old faded notebooks I have found the very year. But that is my own story. From Tobermory Bay, round Ardnamurchan, and up the Sound of Sleat we sailed, all through the livelong day, until in the evening we dropped anchor at Isle Ornsay.

What a run north that was! With a top-sail breeze, and every sail drawing to perfection, so long as the man at the tiller kept his eye on the leech. Moidart, Arisaig, Morar of the white sands, and Knoydart of the lonely sea lochs—Prince Charlie's own land—on the starboard side; with Eigg, Rhum, and the green lands of Sleat on the port. The soft summer wind sang in the shrouds, and the blue seas sweeshed along the lee gunwale in white foam. Climbing the rattlings, I sat on the cross-trees, one arm round the mast, swinging with the plunging ship in perfect happiness, far above the little black people on the deck. The seabirds circled and screamed above the fluttering burgee at the masthead, and I was all alone with my dreams betwixt the sea and the sky.

Yonder was Skye! The dim Coolins rising in serrated loveliness against the blue-white heavens. A whole world of Celtic legendry, romance, and history hidden behind these mighty mountains, and up these sea lochs, and along these shores, which, as yet, I had never visited. Looking back to-day, after many years, during which I have travelled almost every road in Skye, viewed the Hebridean world from a pinnacle of the Coolins, explored the sea lochs, and been drawn back again and again by this island of my heart, I envy the care-free lad who sat on the cross-trees singing to himself as the white-winged yacht raced like a fair adventuress for the island that had never been visited !

This drawing power of Skye for a lover of beauty and old romance must seem almost ludicrous to a practical man who balances his weekly expenses to a penny every Saturday night.

Well do I recall a visit to the town of Wick the very year after my first view of Skye from the cross-trees. I was clad in the sober garments which ten days' residence in that Caithness metropolis required of a Scottish probationer. But, tucked away in a needlessly big bag were some old clothes and an older bonnet. So, when twelve o'clock struck on the Sunday night I ruined all my chances of a " call " back by taking the midnight train—half-luggage and half-passenger—down to Dingwall.

" We'll maybe see you back again," said the old elder who carried my bag.

" Aye," added another, as he shook hands, " and we'll maybe no' ! "

It was a dooms dreich night journey. The autumn frosts had come, and I tumbled out at Dingwall, shivering in the old clothes, as the grey dawn spread over the sky. The Skye train was even slower than the Highland had been. I was really making for Glasgow ! But I was taking the longest possible way in order to get another sniff of Skye. At that time the railway terminus was at Strome Ferry. You scrambled for a meal among a lot of Skye drovers in the Strome Ferry Hotel, and then boarded the Portree boat down at the pier. It was a dismal drizzle of mist and rain all the way. At Portree the real Skye rain gave us a drenching welcome as we walked up the pier. Mountainous seas kept us lively all the way to the Clyde, and when we were rounding the Mull of Kintyre, the salt spray was lashing over the funnel. But it was worth it all. To those for whom the sea has no terrors the salt wind and the crash of great waves make the life-blood dance with joy. And I had seen Skye again !

To-day Skye is being boomed by the Railway Companies, and crowds of tourists can see the island from the inside of fourteen-seater cars, visiting Elgol, and then Coruisk by motor-boat, Dunvegan, and Duntulm, within a few days' time. No part of Scotland is the preserve of the few to-day, except perhaps the wonderful Outer Isles. To one who has sailed the seas, tramped the roads, and climbed the mountains of Scotland for a lifetime, it is harder now than of yore to find silence and solitude and the sleep that is among the lonely hills. This summer there were queues waiting at the door of Dunvegan Castle every visiting day, where long ago one could wander at leisure with the beloved Chief from room to room. Portree on a games day is like a fair. The day was when our only divertisement was to stand in the Square and watch the local volunteers being drilled in their old uniforms.

But it is good that all the world and his wife

B

should look upon the glories of God in nature, so long as they learn to bring to the solitudes a reverent eye and a soul for the mysteries, and a good deal more consideration in clearing away lunch papers, orange peel, and cigarette boxes. There is little fear for the Coolins. These mighty mountains, which from the distance look like the fairy ramparts of heaven, will to the end of the hundred thousand years preserve their desolation from all languid motorists and slipper-footed tourists. Their splintered peaks and far-off corries, their deathly precipices and narrow rock ridges will remain what they have always been—the sanctuary of the strong and the climbers' paradise of peace.

To-day you will find solitude at Trumpan when you dream of Lady Grange and the Battle of the Dykes. Hot silence awaits you among the birch trees and hazels as you wander down the road past Tokavaig to Castle Dunscaith, the home of Sgathach the Warrior Queen, and Cuchullin himself. If the soul of Alexander Smith haunts the old House of Ord with its little pointed windows on Loch Eishort, or the ghost of Sheriff Nicolson revisits Husabost on its way to hear the great Macrimmon play his phantom pipes at Boreraig, the ancient silences will lend them aid to their wanderings. The great seas still thunder about the Neist and Dunvegan Head when the winter gales roar across the Little Minch, and on the quiet summer days there is a heavenly outgate from Bracadale or Snizort to the misty islands that lie asleep on the bosom of the tranquil sea.

The very thought of Skye mingles with my

dreams. For, on those rare occasions when I lie awake, I turn my mind to the Misty Isle, and, beginning at Kyleakin, I travel in fancy over every road in Skye, naming each sea loch and township and clachan as I pass them in my spiritual pilgrimage. A wandering man might well lie awake o' nights for the sheer pleasure of such a fairy jaunt. But by the time I have travelled by far Duntulm or the lonely Point of Sleat, and am footing it wearily past Lusa Bridge for home, the tides of Kyle are racing through the drowsy world of forgetting, where memory is no more, and I am sound asleep.

II

CORUISK

THE LOCH OF MYSTERY

THIS weird loch, lying in a cup of the Coolins, miles remote from the nearest house or travelling road, with a sudden outfall to the sea-waves of Scavaig, is surely the wildest bit of scenery in Scotland.

Not to know Coruisk is not to know Skye.

But how futile it is for anyone to sit down at a table in the far-off city and catalogue the recorded wonders of this savage spot by gathering facts from all the well-known books on Skye, from the diaries of dead travellers, or from the romantic poetry of Sir Walter ! No true lover ever described the face of his beloved in the language of another man. As with faces, so with scenery. We must paint direct, always using our own colours and brushes, the hand obeying the understanding heart which looks out on this wonderful world through a pair of undimmed eyes.

An old photograph lies before me. A group of men standing on the shores of Coruisk in the middle 'nineties. The great adventure had just begun for us all. The lad with the plaid died as the Mayor of a South African town. The tall, dark man with the yachting cap went down with the *Lusitania* when she was torpedoed in the Atlantic. The name of the third man is known in every corner of the world to-day, wherever collectors pick up the finest of etchings. The fourth man, with the blue bonnet, is still exploring the by-ways of Scotland and the highways of the heart. The unseen man who worked the cumbersome, old-fashioned camera has stood before kings, yet has never lost the common touch. Thus, even the loneliest spots on earth are haunted with the ghosts of the past.

It was a June day. We had sailed across to Skye from Loch Scresort, in the Island of Rhum. The laughing summer seas, the sunny deck, the great banks of snow-white clouds floating lazily in the blue, the favouring breeze which made the voyage a sailor's luxury, with the white birds flashing above us and screaming as with delight—it is all as if it had happened yesterday.

Then the mighty Coolins, which always seem so fairy-like from a distance, began to close down upon us with a frown of anger as we entered Loch Scavaig. Slowly we came to anchor, far up in the narrow neck of the loch, where the tiny islands are. A warp was fixed to an iron ring on the rock to starboard, and another to the ring on the rock to port. Then the great seabird folded her white wings, and was at rest for the night.

Standing on the deck, we felt very small in that wild place. Garsven towered above us in all its rocky splendour. The Mad Stream fell down the cliff with a constant hush of mystery. The wind had fallen. In the silence our voices sounded loud and aggressive, as if we were intruding in some other-world preserve of lost souls. Scrambling over

the narrow bastion of rocks which separate the fresh
water of Coruisk from the salt water of Scavaig, we
soon came to the great boulder which is known to
all wanderers round these shores. There, before
us, lay the loch—silent, eerie, grim.

The grassless mountains rose on every side, en-
circling the cauldron of water. There was no sign
of life anywhere. No birds on the naked hills.
No red deer on the slopes of Druim-na-ramh. As
the long summer day declined the gloom settled on
Coruisk—a blue dusk which gradually deepened
into an inky night, making the details invisible.
And yet this ghostly gloom of the Coolins was
exaggerated by the fact that behind that terrific
rampart of rocks the afterglow of sunset was still
shining, and so the long serrated ridge quivered
with sensibility where the inky hills met the luminous
sky.

That night it seemed as if we were living in the
deeps of another world. A star or two came out
in the velvet firmament above the tall masts.
There was something unearthly in the thought of
falling asleep in this abysmal cauldron of Scavaig
to the never-ending husheen of the Mad Stream.
Night at Coruisk is a very different thing from
day. The awful gloom and silence suggest death.

Suddenly there was a quiver of light to the north
above the black hills. Then another, and another,
until the whole sky was illumined with the fires
of the Northern Lights. It was the last touch
needed to give the sense of the unutterable to the
midnight scene, as flash after flash came from the
soundless guns of heaven.

But the next morning we awoke to stern reality. A southerly wind was blowing right into the loch. We had taken our risk, and were now caught in the neck of the narrows. How easy to-day for a sailing boat with an auxiliary motor to face any head wind. But, in the old days, it was all a matter of sails and seamanship against wind and tide. The problem was, how to hoist sail, weigh anchor, and get enough way on to beat out of the narrows on very short tacks, without drifting on the sunken rocks. All hands were at their stations. The anchor was hove short. The bow fell away to catch the wind, but had to be brought up again for the other tack almost before there was any speed on the little ship. It was " 'Bout ship " again and again. Then the inevitable happened. The sea lifted her forefoot, and she began to plunge. At the next plunge she bumped keel on. We had hit a sunken rock. She quivered from stem to stern like a living thing outraged.

Captain Mac rapped out an appropriate sailor word. Every man did what he was told. But the sea-cook—who knew nothing of the way of ships, stood holding on to a rope, as white as one of his own soda scones, with teeth chattering, in a sheer funk. More than one eye calculated the distance it would be to swim ashore at the Bad Step. But at the next plunge, which we all feared, she was in deep water. She gathered way, and laying over to the breeze, she was safe. Within an hour we were racing close-hauled for the Point of Sleat. Such was my first coming to Coruisk.

Years passed, and two men pitched their camp

on the shores of that uncanny loch. They were both artists. For what painter has not longed to make an immortal picture of Coruisk ? Could anyone find a more isolated spot for a dwelling-place ? The Isle of Soay is three miles off by water. To the nearest house at Camusunary it is a good three miles' walk round a desolate shore. Sligachan is eight miles distant across Druimhain, and the track lies down one of the wildest glens in Scotland. I have said that at night the gloom of Coruisk suggests death. It was more than that to the two painters. Death actually came, stalking down the cauldron side like a black shadow. One of them died, and the other was left alone with the body of his friend to people the solitude. Ever since, even on the brightest summer day, Coruisk has been a sinister place to me.

My last visit to Coruisk was but a year or two ago. The day was one of God's poems—all blue and white and sunny. When the rest of the world was deluged with floods of rain, Skye smiled serene in the sunlight. That is Skye. Celestial beyond our dreams when all the world weeps, and wetter than the worst place when the fat Southern shires are sweltering in the sun.

We took the road to Elgol by Broadford and Kil-Christ. Mighty Blaven rose above the green shores of Loch Slapin in all the glory of cliff and corrie and scree. The road hugs the shore round the head of the loch, and from Faolean you look across to fine sheeplands and the long, low nose of Rhu Suisnish ending in a little cliff. Up and up the rough road climbs, over the green moors, and round the shoulders of little Ben Meabost. And from Elgol post office, Eigg, Rhum, and Canna are lying out on the summer seas before you.

The road plunges down a steep hill to the shore. Here the boat lay waiting by the inhospitable beach, with Sandy, Angus, and Donald aboard. In the most out-of-the-way places in Skye you will see men wearing old blue jerseys, which they brought home many years ago after a season of the Clyde yachting. To-day the name of more than one famous yacht adorns the breasts of the Skye boatmen. So it was at Elgol.

The boat had a motor engine, but there is not always comfort in that thought. The engine would not start. After much palaver, we hoisted the ancient brown sail, while Angus and Donald coaxed the engine and kept giving it an unwise number of drinks.

" She will be all right in a minute ; she is only a wee bit ill-natured," was the continual refrain.

Another spate of Gaelic and English about paraffin oil, sparking plugs, and choked pipes.

" She will be all right. We came over from Soay this morning."

Doubtless.

So we held on under sail. But it was slow work.

At last, by one of those lucky chances which even a skilled engineer could scarce explain, the engine got over its ill-temper and became good-natured. That is the delightsome thing about the isles. In spite of everything, you always get there, somehow and sometime.

That day the gloom of Coruisk was wondrously

illumined. The Coolins were sleeping in beauty, without a suggestion of storm or tragedy or death. The outgait to Rhum and Eigg was a perfect dream of pearl and blue. Old days or new, sad memories or gay, here was the indescribable mystery, the solemn grandeur, and a peace that was almost holy.

But the wind was freshening, and the blue sea was now foam-flecked. Angus brought over the boat from the little island to the rocks beside the sandy bay. It was significant that Angus and Donald were still tinkering with the moody engine.

We set out bravely at last, with the motor chugging unevenly, like a long leg and a short. To steady the now plunging boat we determined to hoist the sail. When the old patched canvas was nearly set, I laid my heavy hands on the halliard and hoisted the sail home. The rotten rope broke. Down came the sail and the great spar with a rattle, smothered us all, and hit some on the head. A spate of Gaelic was met by a torrent of English. The boat crashed on through the rising seas under the power of the lame motor. But, despite ill-natured engines and rotten ropes, we got there.

My memories of Elgol that day circle round a splendid tea, a spotless kitchen, and a curious picture of the poet Burns. There is also a vision of a sweet old Highland lady in a pure white mutch, who had no English, and had never been out of Elgol in her long life of eighty-four years. The oleograph portrait of Burns was doubtless a German print. The face was quite recognisable, but the dress was grotesque. He had a plaid over his shoulder, lace ruffles hanging about his wrists, and the delicate, lady-like fingers of a dilettante who had never done a day's work or held a plough.

But these are mere incidentals, like the lame motor and the rotten halliard.

The mystery of Coruisk, like the beauty of old age and the grace of human kindness, remains.

> Blessings be on ye, both now and aye,
>   Dear human creatures!
> Yours is the love that no gold can buy,
>   Nor time can wither.
> Peace be to thee, and thy children, O Skye!
>   Dearest of Islands.

III

HEBRIDEAN MEMORIES

THE LURE OF THE ISLES

There is a strange yearning in the soul of some of us to be always stepping farther westwards towards the lands of the setting sun. I never look out from the shores of Wester Ross but I wish to be on Skye; and I never stand on a mountain-top or headland of Skye but I long to be setting out again for the Hebrides. Nor was I content till I had sailed sixty miles west of these outer isles and set my foot on that lonely rock in the Atlantic—St Kilda. It is the old argument to every wandering man, that when the sun goes down for the last time there must be some land of eternal bliss beyond all the islands and seas of this world.

So once more we stepped on board the old boat and set out from Skye for the Hebrides.

The morning was full of rain. But the glass was rising, and by the time we reached the Crowlins it was clear and dry. Thereafter it was one of God's own days all the way across the Minch to Harris— brilliant sun, blue seas, fine visibility, with pearly views of Skye and the Outer Isles.

We took the outside of Trodday, with the white light on the top, and its two red supply tanks on the cliff below, and set the course for Scalpay. Scalpay is a large green island at the mouth of Loch Tarbet, in Harris, with a population of about 700 souls. I have witnessed many homecomings to Scalpay, for the people there have kind hearts.

I have seen the salmon fishers from the Don and Dee and Tay returning when the fishing season was over—tall, upstanding lads, crowded together in the forecastle, full of merriment and Gaelic joviality. The men all joined hands, and, with the utmost solemnity, kept singing Hebridean croons and songs, swaying their hands and arms to keep the time. When the singing was over, the dancing began, to the music of a melodeon, with reels and steps and hoochs on the plunging boat. They never once lost their feet, nor did the solemnity ever leave their faces. Who shall blame them if they were seriously happy, for they were returning from that mainland world which seldom understands them, to their island home, which is all in all to them.

That day the bell on the Skeirigoe lightship, off Scalpay, sounded eerie on the tumbling waves, and squalls of stinging rain drove across the racing seas, to be followed again and again by sunbursts, which made the desolate hills of Harris look beautiful through the mist.

When we drew near Scalpay, little groups of men and women—mostly women—were standing on the hills and at the crofts, waving a welcome to the salmon fishers. At the pier a great crowd of excited women, with a few old men and boys, stood waiting. When at last the gangway was down and the salmon-fishers, in their good clothes and Sunday hats, stepped ashore, there was great hand-shaking and

kissing. Every man returning seemed to kiss every
girl and old woman present without exception, and
no one seemed abashed. The women joked and
smiled, and there was great Gaelic, but still the
lads never lost their gravity. Then, in twos and
threes, they all went off to their own island crofts.

But to-day we were to witness a very different
welcome. A great lady and her friends were on
board, returning to a castle in Harris. For eleven
years they had been exiles, as the estate had been
bought by an industrial millionaire. Now, after
his death, the estate had been bought back, and the
old proprietor was returning. As we approached
Scalpay we noticed a string of flags on the lighthouse, and through the glasses we read the one
word "Welcome." At every house and croft on
Harris or Scalpay home-made flags were flying and
handkerchiefs were waving. An old *cailleach* stood
on the shore and waved a white clout in each hand.
At Scalpay pier the crowd clapped their hands and
cheered. The boats were all beflagged. The lady
stood on deck, dressed in a felt hat and a tweed
coat closely buttoned up to the neck, and waved a
smiling "Thank you" back. But, to the primitive
mind, great folks are always supposed to be dressed
in gorgeous raiment, and the beloved proprietrix
did not understand a loud remark in Gaelic from a
woman on the pier-head: "Oh, but isn't she awful
plain!"

When we left the pier the sun was shining
brightly on the little run-rigs of corn which creep
like green caterpillars among the rocks of the barren
Harris shores. I never sail up Loch Tarbet but I

gaze at these pathetic pockets of corn among the bogs, and at a roofless grey stone cottage. It was the home of a Harris man who spent his life as a shepherd on one of the Falkland Islands, near the Horn; yet he came back to the old Hebridean home, built this house, and died happy on his own side of the world.

At Tarbet the pier was packed. A piper was playing. The lady, who was also returning to her island home, stepped ashore. Two pipers played "The Mackenzies' March" as she followed them to the pier-head. We all went ashore and heard the doctor's wife make a speech of welcome, to which the lady replied, that they had been very sad to leave eleven years ago, but were glad to return, and proud to be able to speak of "our tenants" once more; for the laird is one who deals gently with the poorest crofter, and mixes a great deal of human kindness with his finance. Would that all our great Highland estates were owned to-day by men who know, and understand, and live among the people of the glens and islands!

At Rodel we saw the ancient church with its square tower—the cathedral of the Outer Isles—where you can look upon the original burial-place and monument of the Macleods. It is a place of mighty rocks, with a little harbour hidden behind them, and as you look at the old church, the barren rocks, and the heaving seas, a sense of old centuries rises up within you. Little wonder that they have called an old tune, "The Rocks of Rodel."

As we sailed south, the whole Hebridean world was shining in beauty. The isles knew neither mist nor rain that day, but lay in the light of the evening sun, like islands of the blessed, all their barrenness softened into tenderness as if no storms had ever riven their grim rocks and arid cliffs.

All the way from Rodel to Lochmaddy there was a glorious westering sun. As we drew into the great bay, past the Maddies, Skye lay in the light of the sunset, its cliffs and headlands steeped in a pink mist. Over the low dark lands of Lochmaddy itself the sun was sinking, the molten ball making the myriad wavelets glitter with golden laughter. The sky was cloudless, and the sunset radiance melted upwards into a green glory which was lost in the deep blue zenith above. When at last the sun dipped, the islands became a deep purple. One little level cloud of gold floated in the sky. The very houses and the masts of the *Claymore* lying alongside of us at the pier were glorified against the sensitive heavens. The memory of many a Hebridean night moves me like an old romance, and no pen can ever describe the haunting sense of beauty that rose within us as we watched the dying of one of these ethereal days among the Western Isles.

By ten o'clock a great crowd of people had gathered on the pier alongside the two steamers. In such a place and at such an hour the whole life of the islands unfolds itself. Friends coming and going, meetings and partings, luggage derricks swinging to the rattle of the donkey engines; the whistle of the busy mate, or the shout of a deck-hand to the men who are working in the dim-lit hold far below. A piper was playing merrily on deck,

as the sheep and cattle and provisions were shipped
or unloaded. An old *cailleach*—a great-grand-
mother, in a black bonnet—sat silent on a box and
nursed a tiny baby, the young mother and the
grandmother beside her—four generations on the
pier-head !—the pang of parting on their faces,
while around them arose the merry shouts and
laughter of the young folks who were now dancing
to the piper. A rosy-faced man in a blue bonnet and
a kilt, intent on nothing but his own merchandise ;
a set of wild-looking tinkers from Rodel ; bread
and drink for the isles, as the deck-hands work un-
concernedly at their heavy tasks, and the sound
of soft voices tell their heart-tales to each other
in the Gaelic tongue that is older than history.
Over all this traffic of the West, with its mingling
of the lonely shielings and the far-off city to which
these soft-tongued, warm-hearted Celts are returning—the blue-black sky, the heavenly afterglow, and
the watching of the first stars !

O island hearts ! so sensitive to every mood of the
sky and sea, to the gloom of storms and the laughter
of the sunshine, to the pipe and dance, and the
ties of home which none can cut without a pang—
our hearts go out to you in the love which always
understands. We share your tears when the old
lament rises with its piercing sobs, and we join in
your laughter round the fire when you throw on
another peat. May the fires of your little black
houses never go out.

The star of evening, like a little lamp of God,
was hanging in the velvet sky when the afterglow
died away. It cast a long silver thread of light

c

across the sea of glass. When at midnight we made for Skye again, all the heaven was strewn with stars. With a wash of seas about us we moved once more through a world of mystery, with a prayer in the heart for every island home that was hushed to slumber beneath the loom of the hills.

IV

THE MAN OF SILENCE

A RAINBOW DAY IN THE FOREST

THERE are days, even in the month of June, when the November-like darkness and a downpour of rain compel a sentimental Scot, whose lot is cast in the haar-haunted city, to manufacture his own sunshine. I suppose the saints could always rise above their surroundings. Those mythical saints! But surely Amiel hit the mark of average humanity when he wrote in his *Journal Intime* that every day is a mood of the soul.

On a day of summer dool like this my heart always goes out to the shining West, and I am thankful that when I close my eyes I only then begin to see. After a summerless June, when we are beginning to wonder if we shall ever see the sun again, I delight to think that on many a western isle the grass is burnt brown on the machairs by the sea because of the long drought and the incessant heat.

    .   .   .   .   .

It was one of those mornings which were too good to last. Summer was dead. The brackens were beginning to splash the hill-sides with spots of russet and gold. Skye was steeped in sunshine from Hunish Head to the Point of Sleat.

The Coolins rose sharp and clear against the

brilliant sky, and the snowy clouds were banked on the horizon with a hint of coming showers. In the early morning the sea had been like glass, and the white clouds repeated themselves in the mirror of the waters.

But, later on, a breeze sprang up, and the glassy sea became one vast expanse of the deepest sapphire.

The white boat was waiting on the edge of the tide, with Donald Mhor tinkering at the engine.

Mike and I stepped on board, and we were soon racing over the blue seas against the wind and tide, with a splash of white spray between us and the sun. We passed Saucy Mary's castle on our way from Kyleakin to Kylerhea.

On such a morning of dazzling beauty the view up Loch Alsh to Duich and the Five Sisters of Kintail is beyond words. But the talk was more of velvet-free horns than of scenery, for Mike was after the first stag of the season, and we fervently hoped that for once Beinn na Cailleach would be free from vagueing tourists.

True to its over-brightness, the morning broke down, and just before we reached the old pier on the Skye side of Kylerhea the first shower swept over us. Mackinnon the stalker met us at the jetty. He was a middle-aged man, with a serious weather-beaten face and a white moustache. There was not an ounce of superfluous flesh on him. There he stood in the rain, silent and alert, quite oblivious to anything but the guns, the luncheon bag, and the work on hand. Weatherwise, and dedicated to deer, he was absolutely detached from the elements

and contemptuous of a shower, as all the islesmen
are.

We sheltered for a little in his house, which was
once the ferry inn. Here I straightway began to
think of the quarrel Dr Johnson had with poor
Boswell on the mainland yonder when they were
climbing the wild zigzags of Ratajan before they
reached Glenelg—that damp and dirty inn which
was furnished with not a single article which they
could eat or drink. I dreamed also of the high
revels which must have taken place in this gaunt
parlour, where we were now sheltering, when this
old road was the only way from Skye to the southern
markets. The room was immediately filled with a
rabble of phantom drovers and herds, and the
sound of lowing cattle and baa-ing sheep came in at
the window.

Then we set off up the old grass-grown road
which climbs the glen above the Kylerhea river,
and joins the Broadford road at Lusa Bridge, seven
miles farther on. Just where the burn comes
tumbling down from Coire an Fraoich, between
Beinn Bhuidhe and Scuir na Coinneach, Mackinnon
left the road, and we followed. Here the real
business of the day began, and from that moment
silence was the order of our going.

I still maintain that few town-dwellers have ever
been quite alone, or know what real silence means.
But a hill-man is bred to silence, and a stalker lives
on it. From eleven o'clock until the evening of
that day we climbed and scrambled and spied without any rest, unless for the half-hour we spent over
lunch. During that time Mackinnon was so intent

on the stalk that he never spoke, only giving an occasional wave of direction with his arm, or pointing out the slot of a deer with his stick. As every stalker knows, there are comparatively few deer on Skye, and no forests of importance; so the very intensity of Mackinnon's silence was all the more humorous.

We climbed to the tops, and crept round Scuir na Coinneach, Beinn na Greine, and Beinn na Cailleach itself; squelching through bogs; skirting some quite respectable precipices; and, on one occasion, slithering damply down a little waterfall —only pausing when Mackinnon wished to have another spy through his long telescope. Sometimes he kneeled and steadied his glass on his stick. Sometimes he lay down on his back, and wriggled his leg round the telescope, twisting his body into every conceivable tortuosity. But there were no stags!

From the top of Beinn na Greine we saw a motor-car party having lunch by the side of the old road far below in the glen, while a dog ranged wildly after some of the picnickers.

" Good-bye to any chance of a stag on this side of the glen ! " I whispered to Mike.

Mackinnon glared, waved his hand contemptuously in the direction of the tourists, shook his head, but never spoke. It was his way of saying unspeakable things. The man of silence then determined to leave the western side of the stalk severely alone, and immediately made over the hill for another beat. We did all the corries on the north side, but still without picking up a beast.

Suddenly we noticed a group of sheep, all bunched together, and moving hurriedly over the ptarmigan ground on the summit. They stopped and looked back as if they had been disturbed by something moving beyond the ridge. But here we drew a blank again, only marking one blue hare.

It must not, however, be supposed that the day was dull or inglorious. A fisherman who has trudged home with an empty basket will know what I mean. The viewpoints were wonderful. With the scudding showers and the blazing sun the day was a dream of blue-grey distances. The circle of vision began with the hills that rise about Loch Eishort. Rhum lay far out at sea, with a puff of white mist on its peaks, making it true to its name, the Altar Isle of the Sea. Loch Slapin slept in sunshine, with mighty Blaven keeping sentinel, and the Coolins were capped with clouds. The great moors behind Broadford lay like a well-laid carpet of purples and browns, dappled in light and shade. The little Isle of Pabbay floated on the inner seas, green as an emerald. Then the eye ranged from Raasay and Rona across to Torridon, Applecross and Lochcarron, Loch Alsh, Loch Duich, with little Loch Long, the Five Sisters of Kintail, Ben Screel frowning above Loch Hourn—the whole panorama is unequalled in Scotland, and on such a day one dreams of heaven, and wonders if it will be half so beautiful! To remember such a view on the dark November days is to thank God for the vision, the silence, and the beauty of the high tops. For,

Who has the hills for friend
Has a God-speed to end
His path of lonely life,
And wings of golden memory to depart.

G. W. Young.

While we were at lunch Mackinnon removed to a distance to brood over his disappointments, so for half an hour we were free to eat and talk and smoke without feeling guilty. I was just waxing eloquent on the tenderness of a well-cooked stag's liver when Mackinnon wandered over to us and quietly lifted the bag with the determined look of a crusader on his face. With the shortest possible number of words he was off again, and, when he led, what could anyone do but follow ?

The showers broke on us again and again. The rain tasted cold on the heights, and rainbows made the western world of sea and mountain a perfect fairyland when the sun blazed out again. Mackinnon was spying on the ledge of a little precipice, and we two sat behind a bluff on the steep face sheltering from the stinging rain. When the shower passed, the most glorious double rainbow of the day was thrown across the corrie, enclosing in its arch the whole of Kintail. Mike and I were spellbound, for it was the most vivid display of the spectrum we had ever seen. But Mackinnon rose slowly from his perch and deliberately turned his back on the rainbow ! He had seen it without a doubt, as indeed he saw everything. But there was something grand about this silent man giving his whole soul to his work. Beauty was well enough in its way. But his one duty was to find a stag for his young master, and nothing in heaven or on earth would turn him aside from his purpose.

So we continued all day, without resting, following Mackinnon, saying nothing, but wondering how this man of silence would feel in the noise of a midland town, or in the crush of a Rugby International at Murrayfield. I can see the picture distinctly at this moment—the silent Celt with the all-seeing blue eyes walking catlike across the rocks with the rifle in its case over his shoulder ; the young sportsman following, tireless, and as keen as youth can be ; while the looker-on in a draigled kilt brought up the rear.

When at last we got down in the evening light to the shepherd's cottage at Rhu na Cailleach, Mackinnon turned round, and with perfect courtesy made his first speech of the day :

" I am very sorry, sir, that you have had a blank day."

That was all. But what else was there to say ?

Donald Mhor was waiting for us in the white boat.

" What luck ? " he cried.

" Two big stags," was the modest reply.

" Yes," added Mackinnon, becoming eloquent for the first time, " and you are to be here at seven o'clock to-morrow morning to go up to the top with me to bring down the big stags to the boat."

" Well, well, well," replied Donald Mhor, his heart sinking at every word, " the doctor has brought you the good luck after all."

But he was a sailor man, and the thought of

climbing up the steep sides of Beinn na Cailleach in the morning to drag down two heavy stags took all the pleasure out of him.

Next morning, however, there were fifteen deer feeding quietly in the part of the forest which we did not spy. Mike made no mistake, and took the stag in the right place. Not many days after that, I was sitting at home in the haar-haunted city eating delicious stag's liver, with a vision of the man who turned his back on the rainbow, and a wish that this noisy world of chatterers would learn a lesson of silence from him and get on with their work.

V

THE BORERAIG BAGPIPE

A PIPER'S PILGRIMAGE

It matters not whether you play like MacCrimmon himself or like a travelling tinker, if there is a touch of Gaelic in the tune and the true swing in the music, you will get a welcome from a Highland heart in any part of the world.

To-day the frost is white on the Lowland fields, and it is a far cry from Auld Reekie to Boreraig. But you have only to put a tune on the chanter, and yonder is Dunvegan Loch sleeping in the sun, with the scent of thyme in the warm winds as you tread the springy turf of the MacCrimmons' parade ground on the Hoe above the sea. Then, peace and war, love and hate, and the hundred thousand battles of the sad old days come marching down the corridors of time. For, from first to last, the piob mhor has set the youkie feet of youth adancing, or sobbed out its coronachs of sorrow—the friend of man in his deeps of dool or his jaunts of brave adventure.

We had come a long way, as every piping loon must, to make the pilgrimage to Boreraig and little Galtrigal. It was a radiant day.

Many a man has asked me why the day is always so fine when I make my way through the haunted glens. And I answer in the word of the old Gaelic saying, "On the fine day take your coat with you, but on the bad day go as you please," which means that the fine days live with us for ever, but the bad days are soon forgot.

So, by Bracadale and Skinidin and Colbost we travelled, until we were beneath the shadow of Macleod's Tables. Dunvegan, hoary with a thousand years of history, stood in the sun across the loch. At Husabost, among the smiling crofts, we thought of Alexander Nicolson—for that great son of Skye was born here—and we passed along the road singing his immortal song :

Jerusalem, Athens, or Rome,
  I would see them before I die ;
But I'd rather not see any one of the three
  Than be banished for ever from Skye.

Then comes the Dun of Boreraig, with Boreraig itself, and the Piper's Cave at Galtrigal a little way along the shore.

This ground is sacred to every piper. The site of MacCrimmon's College is down in that hollow by the shore. On the long flat Hoe above it the pipers used to parade when playing, flinging their pibrochs across the water, while their eyes gazed enraptured on the incomparable view of the Hebrides, far out beyond the loch.

Far be it from me to mar my memory of that day with dates and details of history which every piper knows. It is enough to say that the greatest of all the MacCrimmons was Patrick Mor, who

succeeded his father as hereditary piper to the
Macleods of Dunvegan. It is impossible to say
when the MacCrimmon family came to Skye ; but
tradition says that Alastair Crotach gave the
MacCrimmons their lands at Boreraig ; and Alastair
was chief from 1480 to 1540. Moreover, there are
entries in the estate accounts at Dunvegan of pay-
ments being made to the MacCrimmons up to the
end of the eighteenth century.

What piping must have been heard down there
in the hollow, and up here on the Hoe, during these
centuries ! To the College at Boreraig came pipers
from all parts of Scotland to learn the perfect art
—MacArthurs, Mackays, and Campbells. Patrick
Mor, like all great musicians, put the secrets of his
heart into his playing. His music sprang from his
own sobs, as when he composed the " Lament of
the Children" after seven of his eight sons died
of the fever in one year. So has it been with all
great pipers—the bagpipe was their *amchara* or
soul-friend. Into it they sobbed their griefs,
and out of it came the music of all their battle
passions, their love tragedies, and their brave adventures. It would be easy to illustrate this from
many of the MacCrimmon masterpieces. And yet,
these geniuses had no musical notation such as
we use to-day. They used *canntaireachd*, a kind
of musical shorthand made up of pronounceable
vocables, each of which conveyed a definite note
or grace-note which could be crooned to an air.

Sitting on the Hoe at Boreraig I could almost
hear the long, heart-breaking notes of the lament
—*Cha till mi tuille*, " I return no more," floating

down the wind. Piping to these men was a matter of life and death.

In a fit of jealousy an old Breadalbane piper caught hold of the hand of his brother piper and thrust it into the fire to prevent him becoming a better piper than himself.

The MacCrimmons, who kept all the secrets of their system in their own family, once heard that a girl friend had obtained knowledge of a certain combination of notes and passed the information on to her sweetheart. There was only one way of preventing such a leakage of musical information in the future, so the girl's fingers were cut off.

These things are brought strangely near to me. For, as I write, I am fingering a very ancient, home-made, single-handed chanter which was dug up in a peat-bog near the Chief's house in a glen of bloody memories, and I often wonder, when I handle it, if it did not belong to some one-handed piper who in desperation shaped this rude chanter for his remaining hand!

But pleasanter than these is the legend of the Silver Chanter, which has been told in different forms. A great piping competition was taking place at Dunvegan before Macleod. Naturally the Dunvegan piper was to play last. But, when the playing was nearly over, MacCrimmon was nowhere to be found. Calling one of the Mac-Crimmon lads to him, the Chief sent him to search for the King of Pipers. But, when found, the great MacCrimmon was drunk. Macleod, in despair, then whispered into the boy's ear, "The eleventh piper is just stepping forward, but you

will be the twelfth for your Chief." The lad ran
out to the hill-side in an agony of consternation.
Suddenly a fairy appeared to him from a mound,
and presenting him with a silver chanter bade
him play. The lad did so, and the little glen at
Dunvegan was filled with the divinest piping.
Entering the hall when the eleventh piper was
just finishing, the MacCrimmon lad put the silver
chanter to his lips and outplayed them all.

But piping was not confined to the Highlands of
Scotland. We know that the miller in Chaucer's
"Canterbury Tales" rode on a horse, playing a bag-
pipe with one enormous drone, if the Ellesmere
Manuscript is to be trusted :

> A baggpype wel coude he blowe and sowne,
> And ther-with-al he broghte us out of towne.

Shakespeare speaks of "the drone of a Lincoln-
shire bagpipe" and of people who "laugh like
parrots at a bagpiper." Indeed, it may be news
to an Englishman that the bagpipe was an estab-
lished institution in the life of old England. From
the accounts of the Lord High Treasurer we learn
that the English bagpipers used to visit the Scots
Court, for on 10th July 1489 there is an entry for
payment, "eight shillings to Inglis pyparis that
came to the castle yet and playit to the king."

Stranger still, William of Wykeham in 1403 presented New College, Oxford, with a silver gilt
Pastoral Staff, exquisitely wrought and bejewelled.
It is one of the most gorgeous relics of its kind, and
is usually kept in a glazed recess on the north side
of the chapel. If you look carefully at this ancient

crozier you will notice among the many figures carved on it an angel playing the bagpipes.

Strangest of all, perhaps, is Holbein's drawing (No. 47) in his famous series called "The Dance of Death." Here the Fool is mocking Death by putting his finger in his mouth, and at the same time is endeavouring to strike him. Death smiles and is amused at his efforts, and leads him away in a dancing attitude, playing all the time on a bagpipe which has a chanter and two large drones.

But, indeed, the bagpipe is mentioned in history and literature all down the centuries. From Giraldus Cambrensis in the twelfth century, through the writings of James I., William Dunbar, John Knox, and many others, the bagpipe drones its way. Only in Aberdeen, "that unnatural town," as Samuel Rutherford called it, did the Magistrates prohibit the common piper from going his rounds on 26th May 1630, "it being an uncivil forme to be usit within sic a famous burghe and being often fund fault with."

The most unique bagpipe I ever saw lies in the Museum at Naples. There, among the tragic relics which were found in the buried city of Pompeii, you will find a bagpipe with two little drones and a very small bag, all fossilised, as it had lain for centuries in that lava-covered city. And yet we need not be surprised at bagpipes in Pompeii, for a bagpipe appears on one of the Roman coins of Nero's time.

Every man must be allowed to make his own notes on the history of anything. So, even when sitting in the sun on the Hoe at Boreraig, my thoughts flew to a little collection of photographs of monkish misereres which I possess.

The word " miserere " was at first applied to the Penitential 51st Psalm, which commences with the words " *Miserere mei, Domine.*" Later on the word was applied to the wooden seat in a chancel stall on which the monk sat. Hinges were put on in later times, so that the monk, when he stood up to sing the long service or the penitential psalms, could rest himself on the bulged edge when the seat was hinged back against the stall. On the wood, just below the bulged edge, was invariably carved the grotesque figure of a beast or man. So in the old pre-Reformation cathedrals, abbeys, and churches, these miserere seats provide a humorous instance of how the weary but wily monks managed to sit during a long service when they were supposed to be standing. And who will blame them?

Hinge up these ancient seats, and what will you find? Under one miserere in Beverley Minster a monkey is playing a bagpipe while a bear dances. Under another, in the same church, a pig plays the pipes at the pig trough, while two little pigs look on. A third seat in Beverley shows a monkey imitating a piper by holding a dog inverted under the arm, seizing the hind legs with both hands, and putting the dog's tail in the mouth for a chanter—all to the utter consternation of the dog, which snarls behind the monkey's back. In Ludlow Church a headless demon carries a dishonest pothouse woman to hell to the accompaniment of the bagpipe, and at the other end of the miserere you see her actually disappearing into the pit. In Ripon Cathedral

D

there is a miserere under which is carved a well-groomed pig, with a shingled mane, playing the pipes, to the evident delight of two piglets that gaze entranced at the player. Even when we leave the misereres the bagpipe motive follows us to the carving on wooden screens and the stone sculptured architecture of the cathedral itself. In Exeter Cathedral there is a fine screen in front of the Minstrels' Gallery, with twelve angels playing twelve different musical instruments. The second angel on the left is playing a bagpipe—a sure sign that the music of the pipes was considered to be of heavenly origin! Last of all, high up on the south wall of our own Melrose Abbey there is a gargoyle in the form of a very straight-nosed pig playing the pipes.

From all which we infer that the monks of the Middle Ages, on both sides of the Border, were well acquainted with the bagpipe, that they were humorists of the first water, that the pig was a favourite subject, and that the ancient pipe had only one drone.

When I think of the dog, on the miserere at Beverley, being used by the monkey as a bagpipe, I am reminded of a saying in the Highlands, "There's both meat and music here," said the dog when he ate the piper's bag. And still of another old word, which is surely not of Highland origin, "Bring not a bagpiper to a man in trouble."

Whilst sitting in the blessed sunshine of Boreraig that day, I saw an old man cutting hay with a scythe on a croft close by. The only sound that broke the silence was the rasp of the old man's hone

on his antique scythe.   Eleven sweeshes in the lush
grass, and the mower paused to rest.   Other eleven
sweeshes, and he looked about him again.   I
counted the rhythmic strokes, and the resting
times seemed to grow longer at every pause.   Here,
surely, was the peace, the leisure, and the dreaming
memories of a life from which the adventure had
long since fled.   Then I looked at the site of the
famous piping college by the shore.   The old man
was a parable of what had been and would never be
again.   Had not I seen MacCrimmon's pipes lying
in a case at Dunvegan ?   The wail of his own
lament seemed to be wafted across the loch on the
warm winds that whispered about the ears :

> Cha till mi tuille . . . I come again
> no more.

VI

THE FINEST ROAD IN SKYE

FROM KYLE TO DUNVEGAN

IF I had but one day to spend in Skye, and only one road to travel, I am in no doubt about what that road would be. In this age of hurry people are taking their pleasures in tabloid form. I suppose it is inevitable. Crowds arrive at Kyle every summer day and look across the narrow strait waiting for the ferry to carry them over the sea to Skye. Whether they bring cars with them or only a stout stick and a rucksack, their only thought is to see as much of the magic Isle as they can in the shortest possible time. I do not blame them. For one glimpse of the Coolins, even from a distance, sanctifies a summer, as the sight of a lover's face will always be worth a whole day's journey.

But let none think that they will ever surprise the secrets of Skye in that way. Even those of us who have known the island for the best part of a lifetime, sailed its sea lochs, walked its lonely roads, and stood on its highest pinnacle, are still waiting for a longer acquaintance before we can begin to set down our tale of love. But the best love stories in the world will never be written.

Kyleakin is the doorstep of Skye. You are no sooner in the ferry-boat than you are gazing at a little row of white cottages on the farther shore. Westward, up the Kyle, the lighthouse gleams on its island, with the dim blue hills beyond. Eastward, down the Kyle, lies Loch Alsh with its glorious tumble of hills. Right in front of you stands the ruin of Castle Moil on its rock. This keep was built by a Danish Princess—Saucy Mary, the sailors called her, for she stretched a chain across the Kyle and took toll of every ship that passed. For centuries the Mackinnons owned it.

Kyleakin is the pleasantest of all the Skye villages. But, however fair the doorstep may be, it is not the whole house. It may seem but a commonplace row of cottages from the mainland, but the finest thing about Kyleakin, with its green machair and its little tidal ob, is the view out of it. You are no sooner out of the village and across the ravine of the Alt Anavaig, on the road to Broadford, than the Coolins rise before you far away across the little moss haggs of the moor. At Lusa Bridge the old coach road to Kylerhea turns off to the left—a fine six-mile walk for a summer day. Then for some miles you pass through the prosperous townships of Breakish, and you are at Broadford with the Red Hills rising before you.

I never pass through Broadford but I think of Samuel Johnson at Coirechatachan, and Alexander Smith at the Cattle Fair.

The ruins of Coirechatachan lie across the river beneath Ben na Cailleach, one of the Red Hills. A poor rickle of stones now, but once the hospitable home of Mackinnon, who was Johnson's host. Here Boswell got drunk on the Saturday night, and brought down on himself Johnson's heavy rebuke. But there was more than drink going at Coirechat- achan. For, later on, Johnson was seen whispering to Corrie's wife, who immediately cried out: "Oh, I am in love with him!" After which the great man kissed her hand.

Then one of the married ladies in the company actually sat on Johnson's knee, put her arms round his neck, and kissed him.

"Do it again," said he, "and let us see who will tire first!"

If poor Bozzy's head could not stand the High- land whisky, what of Dr Johnson, who, when he was in Edinburgh, drank nineteen cups of tea in the house of Dr Blacklock, the blind poet, much to the consternation of his hostess! Skye is full of the reminiscences of his visit. Over yonder in Raasay he was particularly happy, and on the top of Duncaan, Boswell danced a reel with the rest.

Just a little way down the Ardvasar road, at the Market Stance of Strolamus, Alexander Smith, the author of the finest book on Skye, once attended a cattle fair with his host, young M'Ian of Ord. When M'Ian and he were driving off at the end of the day they came on John Kelly, one of the Ord shepherds, snoring in the heather. Nothing could rouse him.

"We must take him on his fighting side," said M'Ian, whose knowledge of human nature was infinite.

So he shouted into John's ear, "Here's a man from Kyle who says he's a better man than you."

"Tell him to strike me," growled the shepherd.

" Kick him as hard as you can," whispered M'Ian to Smith. And Smith kicked.

John sat up instantly and struck out.

" Catch him now ; his rage has sobered him ; he'll be drunk next minute ; get him into the dog-cart at once."

And this is how they got John Kelly of the child-like heart home.

While wandering about the fair, Smith remembered Johnson's visit to Coirechatachan, and set out alone to visit the shrine. He never reached it, but mistook another ruin for it. But, what does it matter ? These three men—Samuel Johnson, James Boswell, and Alexander Smith—by their inimitable writings, were the first who really made Skye a famous place of pilgrimage, and their ghosts haunt the island still.

The way from Broadford to Sligachan is now made easy for the most fastidious motorist by the new road which skirts the shore from Dunan to Sconser. It is all very smooth and of an easy gradient. But only those who have trudged up the old steep road, across the hills from Dunan to Luib on Loch Ainort, and then from Kinloch Ainort through the wilds of Lord Macdonald's forest beneath the gloom of Glamaig to Sconser Lodge at the mouth of Loch Sligachan, can ever appreciate the solitude and grandeur of this region.

At Sconser may still be seen one or two black houses, with the peat reek coming from the wooden chimney in the thatched roof and through the open door. On the roof of one of these black houses I once saw a man sitting, idly contemplating the universe, after the manner of the Celt. For the roof was simply a continuation of the hill-side, like so many of the old black houses I used to see in Harris thirty years ago. It was at Sconser Inn that the island chiefs met Clanranald, Prince Charlie's messenger, in 1745. But, to the consternation of the Jacobites, Macleod would not " come out."

The little fisherman's hut at the burn-mouth before you come to Dunan, is an ideal cabin made of wood, with a stone-built fireplace. It always reminds me of the hut in which Thoreau wrote his " Walden." Here might a solitary live in peace, think high thoughts, and live on sea trout.

The glorious colour of the sea wrack at the head of Loch Ainort when the tide is far out, great stretches of ochres and umbers and madders, with splashes of bright green sea grass, make a perfect painter's palette on the shores of this lonely little loch.

There is a beautiful view of Raasay House and the open Sound from this point, with a glimpse of the Old Man of Storr far away to the north. It seems like a millennium of years since I first sailed up that Sound, with the fresh breeze filling the white sails and never a flutter at the leech.

To-day the whole of Skye is clear of clouds. But I remember a day here when I saw the search-light of the sun piercing the lowering clouds and sending its spotlight racing along the gloomy hill-side. At the end of the loch there is an old *caraidh*, or fish weir, which is a horse-shoe curve of stones set in the shallow water to catch the fish when the tide recedes. You will find remains of these primitive fish dams all round the shores of Skye. A packman, carrying his whole stock-in-trade on his back, is trudging along with the natural solemnity of one who has more time for meditation than the average shopman of the towns.

To lovers of Skye Sligachan means—the Coolins hemming you in with all their silent mystery; Glamaig and little Marsco for ever in your eye, with Scuir nan Gillean at the back door; the old grey bridge over the Sligachan river, which tumbles down the glen eternally; rain and mist; and the burning heat of a summer sun when all the world of islands and seas is spread below you like the map of God, as you stand on the summit rocks and gaze spellbound.

There are no facilities at Sligachan for the towny tourist. It will never become a motoring centre. The atmosphere of the Inn suggests nothing but ice-axes and fishing-rods, and the comfortable peace of wise men who linger long in this climbers' paradise to exercise their natural gifts of mind and muscle.

No man knows Skye who does not know the Coolins. They draw the eye from almost every Hebridean isle, and get at the heart of mountain lovers as no other hills in Britain ever will. Whether you have the skill to climb their beetling rocks, or only wander round the corries which seem to be bastioned by the walls of the primeval world, or approach them from Loch Scavaig or Loch Brittle, or penetrate their sanctuaries from Sligachan itself, the Coolins must ever remain the preserve of man in all the glory of his strength.

When you leave Sligachan, instead of going north

to Portree by Glen Varragill, keep straight on past the end of the Inn on the road that leads to the west. The jagged ridges of the Coolins are soon left behind, and the green moors of Drynoch are all about you, dappled with cloud and sunshine. Grassy Drynoch of the fine sheep walks is a great contrast to the wilderness about Sligachan. But, that is Skye. A place of sudden changes and great contrasts. From rain to sunshine, from cloudy gloom to heavenly radiance, from the uttermost desolation to the greenest hills. Over the face of this dearest of islands mist and sunlight chase each other like laughter and tears on the face of a little child.

Yonder across Loch Harport is the Talisker Distillery. I can still hear as in a dream the lilting voice of the Highlander describing the triple process of distilling to some American friends as we wandered from vat to vat. But the refrain was always the same—" And the third time it is whuskey ! " That is all I picked up about the making of whisky, and still in my sleepless hours, when I lie and think of Skye, I hear only one sound on the winds of Carbost—" And the third time it is whuskey."

Is there any sea loch in Skye that can sparkle with more heavenly laughter after rain than Loch Bracadale ? If it is a blue day when you pass that way you will see the Hebrid Isles lying like clouds on the rim of the ocean, and great beauty lying over Bracadale, with the Isles of Wiay, Tarner, and Harlosh floating like Viking ships in the bay. Macleod's Tables dominate the landscape to the west, and Macleod's Maidens stand up in the sea at the Point of Idrigil. Huge headlands guard the entrance to the loch. To landward the low green hills are dotted with sheep and cattle. It is all crofts, peat reek, yellow sands, and red wrack round these tidal shores.

The ruins of the broch—Dun Beag—stand near Struan. Dr Johnson, when staying at Ulinish, visited this dun and enlarged on the fact that in Skye "there is an ambition of exalting whatever has survived memory." He also recorded the fact that "Mr Boswell caught a cuddy." The little children of Skye were laughing at their play when we passed the sunny hayfields of Struan. But the brave sons of Skye who have made the traditions of the Misty Isle are scattered to the ends of the earth, and sleep soundly in their foreign graves. No more for them the scent of the peat reek or the sound of the wintry seas.

At the head of Loch Caroy we boiled the kettle, and sat by the roadside near the derelict chapel of St John the Baptist. This plain little Episcopal chapel by the side of the tree-clad ravine always intrigues me, for it seems to speak of an alien faith in a strange land. The seats are all gone. The windows are in a perilous state. A white cross lies across what must have been a simple altar. Even the graves outby record the names of alien sojourners who worshipped God after the manner of their forefathers—Scott, Porteous, Gibbon. Now the wall is crumbling. There is a padlock on the gate. The grass is all tangled, and the trees are overgrown. When I came out again

the tide had receded in the little loch. Ichabod !
Here, too, is a tale that has been told.

It is not far from the Caroy burn to Dunvegan.
You have scarcely left the last waters of Bracadale
at Pool Roag when you see Dunvegan Loch airting
out to the sunset. The castle is the Mecca of all
who come to Skye. But Dunvegan is so great a
sight that it brooks no mere mention at the end of
a traveller's story. So the long day's journey must
end in the old Kirkyard of Kilmuir at Dunvegan.

Here is the burial-place of the chiefs of Macleod
—fit resting-place for so great a succession. It
stands on a hill with a wide view of the Tables, a
burn whimpling past, spleenworts in the ruined
walls, and a multitude of sad old graves. Conspicu-
ous among them is the Lovat pyramid, raised in
memory of Thomas Lord Lovat, who married a
Macleod. He was the father of the notorious
M'Shimi of the 'Forty-five, and he died in 1699.
The inscription, which is now almost obliterated,
drew forth a sneer from Dr Johnson, who said it
was " poor stuff, such as Lord Lovat's butler might
have written."

But all opinions seem small when we wander
among the graves of dead men, and when the sun
goes down the day's cares are soon forgotten.

VII

SLEAT-OF-THE-WAVES

THE GARDEN OF SKYE

THERE are a great many Gaelic proverbs about Sleat, and, strange to say, most of them are about women! Russet Sleat of the Fine Women; Sleat Wives Worth Having; Sleat of the Talkative Ones. These are a few. Even Duncan Ban, who got his wife from Sleat, speaks proudly of her as being of the seed of the Sleat dwellers. I suppose it means that the merits of any district depend largely on its womenfolks. Or is it something else? Be that as it may, Sleat is a pleasant place of low hills, green fields, bird-haunted woods, and sheltered shores. When you take the road to Sleat, you turn your back on the wild region of the Coolin and your face to a fair-favoured land.

The Ardvasar road strikes due south a little east of Broadford, and crosses a region of great moors. Water lilies float like snowflakes on the blue waters of the Lochan Dubh, and as you look across the black tarns these rare blooms seem all the more beautiful because they are so inaccessible. Here, and later on at Loch nan Dubrachan, the old legend of the Water Horse is called to mind, for in every other Highland loch the dreaded *each uisge* used to appear in the mouth of a winter night when the

61

half-lights of the gloaming made the moors an eerie place to stray in.

As you travel on you catch a glimpse of the head-waters of Loch Eishort, the blue tops of Rhum, and the furrowed brow of Blaven. Nearer at hand the Red Hills dominate the moors. And still the landscape opens out at every mile. Little Lochan-a-Daal, with its red sea wrack and its lodge of Kinloch snuggling beside a bouquet of trees. Isle Ornsay right in front of you. The mainland mountains of Loch Hourn across the Sound, with Ben Screel lording it over the whole landscape. Here are green fields and the delightful gardens of Duisdale House, with prosperous crofts, and farther on, the deep-gladed woods of Armadale. Indeed, the low lands of Sleat, seen from the mainland on a sunny day in harvest time, look as if they were covered with a tartan plaid of green and yellow checks. Little wonder that Sleat-of-the-Waves has been called the Garden of Skye.

Behind Isle Ornsay the sailor can always find good harbourage. It holds many pleasant memories for me. I still remember that our skipper, Captain Mac, called the place R'onsay, and as I had never been there before, I could not remember any place in Skye of that name. Now, long afterwards, I know that his sailor's pronunciation of R'onsay was nearer the mark than I then realised. For this island, despite the fact that there are the ruins of an ancient chapel on it, is not named after Saint Oran, like the Island of Oronsay which lies off Colonsay. Both of those islands are called after saints—Colonsay after Columba and Oronsay after Oran.

But the word Ornsay is a place description pure
and simple. The island is called in Gaelic Eilean
Diarmid or Diarman, which easily becomes Eilean
Tiarman, a corruption of Eilean Tioram or Dry
Island. Now, *tioram* is the Gaelic equivalent for
the Norse word *oras-ey*, which means Ebb-tide
Island. So Isle Ornsay is the island that is connected with the mainland at low tide—a very exact
description of the place. A long rigmarole about
Isle Ornsay, doubtless, but it all goes to show that
" unto him that hath shall be given "—although
even a saint should not have more islands called
after him than he has a right to.

I can well remember an excursion that June night
to a croft on the Ardvasar road, in order to buy a
hen. We did buy one, but we had to take it away
alive, as there was none at the croft at that moment
who could thraw the neck of the poor creature. So
I carried the living hen with some trouble into Isle
Ornsay post office, and there, while I was trans-
acting business with the postmistress, the hen ran
off. There was great cackling in the village street
that evening, and the race was not altogether to the
swift. So small a thing will linger in the memory
for a lifetime when greater things are altogether
forgotten.

The road cuts inland across a purple tongue of
land for three or four miles, and joins the sea again
at Knock Bay and the prosperous township of
Teangue. This is just the old Norse word *tunga*,
so well known in Sutherland as Tongue. Here,
on a little rocky knoll by the sea, stands the ivy-
covered ruin of Knock Castle, sometimes called

Castle Camus. This keep was for a long time a residence of the Macdonalds of the Isles. In the reign of James IV. the Macleods laid siege to it, but the siege was raised by a brave woman of Clan Donald, who was ever after called Mairi 'Caistiel. Like all ancient keeps, Castle Camus was haunted. The gruagach's stone is still pointed out, but in this case the *glastig*, or Green Lady, turned out to be a she-devil who appeared in the form of a grey goat.

Another mile and you reach one of the holy shrines of Skye—the old ruined Kirk of Sleat, which is called Kilmore. Surely the war memorial of Sleat has an unrivalled stance on the green knoll near the kirk, with an outlook across the waters of the Sound to the mountains of Knoydart !

In this old kirkyard I have often lingered. The beauty of the place literally compels you, when the wind blows in from the sea and whispers eternal secrets to you as it rustles through the leaves of the immemorial trees. Close by the ruin stands the new kirk. The whole place is a perfect poem—the vista through the Norman east window, the view of Knoydart and the sea, the ancient monuments of the Macdonalds who lie well happed under the old turf, the tree-embowered road outby, and the song of a robin as it sits in the September sun and chants the low, sad song of man's mortality.

Here, doubtless, long ago there was a pagan place of worship. Thereafter, on the same site, a Celtic monk would set up his little cell of Christ. But the first church was built by a priest called Crotach Mac Ghillie Gorm—the Hunch-backed Son of the Blue Servitor, and a Canon of Beauly. This good man

MISTS ON ALASDAIR

travelled all the way across Scotland to preach
Christ to the wild men of Skye. His primitive
church stood at Kilmore until some time in the
seventeenth century, when the Macleods fought a
battle with the MacIntyres in a neighbouring field.
When the MacIntyres were defeated, they sought
refuge in the church, which, like all churches at that
time, had a thatched roof. The Macleods locked
the door, set fire to the thatch, and destroyed
church, MacIntyres, and all. A second church was
built by Macdonald of Sleat in 1691, but, according
to Ian Lom, the Lochaber Bard, the Chief never
saw it finished :

> To the church of Sleat-of-the-Waves
> Its cost you defrayed to build,
> Though you did not wait to slate it.

This church was used for worship until 1876, and
it is now the most beautiful of all the ruined kirks
in Skye.

Armadale Castle is a thing of yesterday. When
the guns of Waterloo were silenced, the masons
began to build this modern castle of the Macdonalds
in Skye.

But it was in a small house at Armadale that
Dr Johnson and Boswell were entertained in 1773
by Sir Alexander Macdonald, the first Lord Macdonald of Slate, in the peerage of Ireland (1776).
He was a very accomplished man and loved music.
Indeed, he composed a number of strathspeys and
reels which are still popular, such as " Lord Macdonald's Reel," " Mrs Macleod of Raasay," " Mrs
Mackinnon, Corry," etc. He was a first-rate

E

violinist, and on one occasion entertained O'Kane, the celebrated Irish harper, to whom he gave a beautiful old harp key which had been long in his family, and was said to be worth eighty or a hundred guineas. It was "made with gold and silver, and set with a precious stone."

Lord Macdonald was a writer of Latin verses and a member of the Society of Antiquaries. The house in which he lived at Armadale in 1773 was only that of a tenant, because the family mansion had been previously burned. His entertainment may have been very frugal, as, indeed, a scholar's often is. But both Johnson and Boswell abused his hospitality unpardonably by holding up their host to ridicule for his poverty. Johnson actually complained in a letter to Mrs Thrale "that he had disgusted all mankind by injudicious parsimony" . . . "that he had no cook" . . . and "that Boswell was very angry." Boswell himself, however, makes this illuminating remark in his Journal —"I had felt a return of spleen during my stay at Armadale."

Why was it that these two travellers spoke of their Highland host so ungraciously? It would almost seem as if Boswell had influenced Johnson against their host. But Dr Johnson did not know what we now know—that Boswell had been an unsuccessful suitor for the hand of Miss Diana Bosville, the very Lady Macdonald who was doing her best to entertain him! This fact may have accounted for his own acknowledged attack of spleen. Moreover, had Dr Johnson known that, he would probably have restrained himself from foolish taunts, and been a more gracious guest when Bozzy was inclined to be nasty at Armadale. The remarks of both about their host at Armadale will not be found in any modern edition, as they only appeared in the first editions of the two Journals, and were subsequently omitted as being altogether improper.

The woods of Armadale are now deep-gladed and luxuriant. The great trees stand in park-like lands, and sweep the ancient turf with their green skirts. Auricarias and rhododendrons flourish here. Indeed, you might think you were wandering through an English demesne of sylvan beauty were it not for the fact that the windows of the grey castle of the Macdonalds are winking in the sun at the wild mountains of Nevis across the sparkling seas.

Then comes homely Ardvasar, with its crofts, its bien houses, and its harvest fields. From Ardvasar it is an up-and-down road all the way to the Aird of Sleat, where a little church stands four-square to every wind that blows, looking right across the open seas to Eigg of the Songs and the white sands of Morar. I have lit my fire on that glamorous road that leads to the end of everything.

But Ardvasar itself is a place of large leisure. On one occasion I chapped at the inn door and asked for tea. A little time after that I saw a woman gathering sticks to light the fire. So we began to explore the by-ways of Ardvasar in the sun, when lo ! we found that the hedgerows were hanging with the most luscious brambles. To this day I wonder if there are any brambles in the world so large and succulent.

After tea I smoked a meditative pipe over the inn library. Among the old books I found the following :

"Calvin's Institutes in Latin." Edited by Tholuck. Berlin, 1834.

"The Liquor Laws of Scotland." By David Dewar.

"Historical Collections, Relating to Remarkable Periods of the Success of the Gospel, and Eminent Instruments Employed in Promoting it." 1754.

"A Greek Grammar." 1831.

Latin, Greek, Whisky, and Religion—these four books seemed to form a synopsis of the scholarship, the conviviality, and the principles of the eighteenth-century lairds whom Dr Johnson met in Skye. For, despite Lord Macdonald's poverty, Boswell was good enough to advertise to the world that the laird of Armadale " had been an Eton scholar, and being a gentleman of talents, Dr Johnson had been very well pleased with him in London."

.   .   .   .   .

O Sleat-of-the-Waves. Far away in a city of the south, when the winter storm thrashes on the window-panes, and the rain-swept streets hold in them no beauty that the eye can see, I sometimes dream of the old ivy-covered Kirk of Sleat at Kilmore, sleeping in the sunshine among the trees, with the blue waters of the Sound gleaming like the crystal sea betwixt the shores of Skye and the ethereal mountains of Knoydart. And—my heart turns within me.

VIII

CASTLES IN SKYE

DUNSCAITH : DUNTULM : DUNVEGAN

CASTLES in Skye! The very thought inflames the imagination. A castle in the Hebrides is not like a castle in the south. These ancient castles in Skye—with one exception—are grim ruins standing on rocky cliffs or headlands looking out to sea. Built for defence in the dim days of old, their stark walls defy the storms that rage around their sodden sites, and every stone is lashed by the spindrift that blows like smoke across the tumbling seas. They have been crumbling for centuries ; yet, for all their fallen strength, they are the true historians of the Isles, and the legendry of a thousand years blows about their lichened walls like the sough of summer winds.

There are at least fifty Duns in Skye—that is, little rocky mounds which are crowned with the foundations or the ruins of brochs, fortresses, or castles. Even the oldest castle stands on the site of a still older broch or tower. A whole volume could be written about these ruins, and to visit each would entail an arduous journey by land and sea round the whole seaboard of Skye.

But no man can ever get at the real romance of a country by sitting at home and wading through the history books. He must take the road for himself and see all its wonders with his own eyes. If you would surprise the secrets of the isles, the sun and the rain must have kissed your cheeks in many a day's adventure, and the good Gaelic must have sounded in your ears like the overcome of an old song whose ending no man will ever know.

Of all the castles in Skye, the three greatest are Dunscaith, Duntulm, and Dunvegan.

As you travel south from Isle Ornsay, you come to a gate on the right-hand side of the road just beyond Loch nan Dubrachan. Open the gate, and there lies before you a rough road that cuts across the promontory of Sleat for five miles to Ord on Loch Eishort. Here the moors are low-lying and green. After passing Loch Meoble and before coming to the trees on the right, the road takes a plunge down a stony hill and then through a tree-clad gorge. Here you get your first view of Blaven. At this spot I met two very large flocks of black-faced sheep, with ten drovers and their dogs, and I immediately thought of old M'Ian, young M'Ian, and Alexander Smith, who must often have passed this way. The road has a desperate surface of rough stones, and there is a great buttress of rock near the sheep fanks. Then comes Ord House, with its little pointed windows, and three dormers in the roof. It is a comfortable homestead standing on a knoll above the sea, and sheltered by a clump of trees.

Ord looks straight to Blaven across the sparkling seas. Here M'Ian, an islesman of the old school and a hardy veteran of the wars, lived with his family in the early days of the nineteenth century. At that time a tacksman in Skye was a kind of Shepherd King. M'Ian was over eighty years of age, of a slight wiry figure, with a fresh complexion and a crown of snow-white hair. As a soldier he had carried colours in Ireland at the end of the eighteenth century. He fought with Moore at Corunna, lifted his gallant leader when he was wounded, and saw the light of pleasure in his dying eyes when the Highlanders charged. He followed Wellington all through the Peninsular Campaign, and was himself wounded at Quatre Bras. At Waterloo he stood in a square that crumbled but never flinched. Then, like countless numbers of old soldiers, M'Ian retired to his beloved Highlands and took a tack of land in Skye. He was a master of legendary lore, an expert genealogist, and an enthusiast in Gaelic poetry. But he was so quick of temper that contradiction drew fire from him like steel from flint. He would let fly a volley of oaths at a careless servant one moment, and the next be bowing his white head most reverently as he knelt at evening prayers. Such was Alexander Smith's hospitable and most human host at Ord. Smith married a M'Ian in 1857, and in 1865 published his "Summer in Skye." My edition (1866) is adorned with a rather crude frontispiece of the "View from M'Ian's House," showing an old boat on the green shore, the blue waters of Loch Eishort, with mighty Blaven rising from the shores of Slapin like a pink and purple cockscomb, and a peep of the blue Coolins beyond.

It was a perfect August day, and the peace of

God lay over Skye. The road from Ord to Tokavaig and the old castle of Dunscaith is rough and steep. As I trudged through the woods of hazel and birch, in the sweltering heat, it seemed that every day in this quiet place must be a Sabbath. Here was a world of silence, sleep, and beauty, with but one sound—the far-off bleat of a sheep. This road continues past Dunscaith to the next township of Tarskavaig, and so leads you back across Sleat to Ostaig and Kilbeg on the Sound.

The desolate ruin of Dunscaith stands on a square bluff by the shore. But what seems an innocent-looking bluff from a distance is really an isolated rock on the north side of a little bay called Ob Gauscavaig. This precipitous rock rises forty feet sheer from the sea on three sides. On the landward side it is cut off from access by a deep gully which is spanned by two arched walls over which there must have been at one time a drawbridge. A flight of stone steps turning to the left rises from the end of the bridge and enters the ruined wall of the castle. Crumbling walls, grass-grown foundations, a beetling rock, traces of an old well, and a glorious view seawards—that is what anyone may see at Dunscaith to-day.

But the glamour of the place will only fall over those who know something of the legendry of Fingal and his heroes, for the poetry of Ossian broods over this wild rock like a sea mist that is shot with sunlight.

It is impossible to thread out the various legends which connect Cuchullin with Dunscaith, and one has to choose between many tales. But it is told that Cuchullin came in his youth from Erin over the waves to Dunscaith to learn the arts of war which were taught there by Sgathach the Terrible, who was Queen of Skye. That must have been in the far-off days of Celtic occupation, for it was Columba who first forbade women to fight in battle. This ruthless Princess had five score of warrior women in her college of arms, and these Amazons on one occasion executed fifty sea rovers by tying the long hair of each to the bough of an oak tree. There the miserable men hung till they died. One of these warrior women was Maev the Strong.

Cuchullin fell in love with Sgathach, the beautiful queen of battle whom the Celts called Bragela, which means the Fair Bosomed. Although fierce in warfare, she was passionately fond of music, possessing a three-stringed harp of magical powers —one string being tuned to laughter, a second to weeping, and a third to sleep. Cuchullin called the queen his Tender Tutoress. And indeed she must have been tender as well as terrible, for she loved him dearly, and having that second sight which is always lengthened by love, foresaw his death in Erin.

So Ossian sings : " O strike the harp in praise of my love, the lonely sunbeam of Dunscaith. Strike the harp in praise of Bragela . . . spread now thy white sails for the Isle of Mist and see Bragela leaning on her rock. Her tender eye is in tears, and the winds lift her long hair from her heaving breast. She listens to the winds of night to hear the voice of the rowers, to hear the song of the sea, and the sound of thy distant harp. And long shall she listen in vain. Cuchullin will never return."

O Dunscaith! What care I though Maclean of Duart or Macdonald of Sleat lived here in later times! My thoughts always fly back to those dim days when Cuchullin and his heroes sailed in their galleys betwixt Erin and Skye. When Bragela of the Fair Bosom looked in vain across the darkling seas for the hero of her heart who was never to return. Did not Cuchullin chain his hound Luath to yonder stone? And do the old wrinkled sennachies of Skye not tell you yet that he is hunting with his dogs when the storm roars among the hills?

"Call," said Fingal, "call my dogs, the long-bounding sons of the chase. Call white-breasted Bran, and the surly strength of Luath."

From Dunscaith to Duntulm is a far cry, and you have to travel the whole length of Skye from Cuchullin's castle till you reach the ancient stronghold of the Macdonalds of the Isles. But every step of the journey brings you some new wonder of beauty or lore.

North of Portree, none but a Londoner will expect a boulevard. But the very roughness of the road secures the peace of the whole seaboard that lies to the east of the great ridge of Trotternish. First come the black splintered precipices of the Storr, with that mighty obelisk which is known as the Old Man of Storr. Only those who have sketched the Old Man from every angle know what a many-sided character he is. The picturesque gorge of Tote, with the now disused Diatomite

workings, and the little derelict railway that led to
Lealt in the moors. Culnacnock, where the local
postman goes his rounds on a long-tailed brown
pony, and you can see the level strata of sandstone
below the upright pillars of volcanic rock on a little
hillock on the right-hand side of the road. Then
Staffin Bay, with its lovely sweep of sand, and
Staffin Island lying in the lap of the sea. Here
there is a multitude of crofts, and the whole world
of Staffin is dominated by the gigantic flat table of
the Quirang, flanked by its pillared cliffs. It will
pay you to turn up the road to Uig and see the old
graveyard of Kilmaruy. All the way north there
are superb views across the sea to the tumbled
mass of the Ross-shire hills, and at Tote there is
a fine backward view to the now far-off Coolins.
But when you cross the northmost tip of Skye, by
Kilmaluag, the outlook suddenly changes and you
are gazing westward over the sea to the dim blue
hills of Harris, with the rugged ruin of Duntulm
Castle standing up on its green hill like a grim
sentry in the foreground of the whole panorama.

This Gaelic word describes Duntulm with complete exactitude :

> Ged tha thu 'n diugh 'a d'aibheas fhuar
> Bha thu uair 'a d'aros righ.

> Though thou art to-day a ruin cold,
> Thou wert once the dwelling of a king.

For Duntulm was the ancient seat of the Macdonalds. Their chiefs were Kings of the Isles, and
proudly challenged the reigning Kings of Scotland.

But this is not the place to enter upon a genealogy which a perfervid Macdonald will assure you goes back to that High King of Ireland, Conn of the Hundred Battles, and even to Breogan the twenty-third in descent from Japhet! That feud is certainly not for my claymore.

Like all these ancient castles, Duntulm was built on the site of a Viking fortress, called Dun Dhaibidh, or the Dun of David, after the hardy Norseman who seized the place. That Norse castle in turn was doubtless built on the site of a still older Celtic fort, and these Celtic forts take us back beyond all the records of history.

Duntulm, true to its name, is *Dun Tulm nam baideal arda*—Duntulm of the High Tower. It is a castle that sits high on a knoll by the sea, with a steep green approach from the landward side, and a fifty-foot drop of rocky cliff to the waves on the other three sides. So it was impregnable from the sea. The usual protecting ditch was cut on the landward side to a depth of fifteen feet, but over this ditch has been raised a broad track in later times to make an easier approach.

It is all a dream of ruined walls, waving grasses, whispering winds, and infinite horizons. The old chamber with the barrel roof, an aumbry at one end and a fireplace at the other. The rugged remains of the old tower. The fascinating view of distant Harris seen through the sea-gate in the northern wall. The little isle of Tulm in the bay, with the masts of a wrecked ship still thrust above the water. The black inhospitable shores, with the deep groove in the flat of the rock down yonder, which has been worn by the keels of the chiefs' galleys—it all brings back the ancient life of the isles whose records were written in blood by the point of many a sharp sword.

Almost under the shadow of the castle walls, on Rhu Meanish, is the Hill of Pleas, or local judgment seat, where the chief administered the clan laws. It is an oval mound about three feet high with a slight rim round the top. How often I have sat on one of these Justice Mounds in the Highlands and thought of the poor wretches who were led away to the chief's gallows close by!

But the wind is sweeshing through the long grasses, and round the ruined walls, like the sighing of the spirits of the dead who are loth to leave their earthly haunts. The summer world is so wonderful that the white lighthouse on Scalpay away over by Harris can be clearly seen. The quiet fields behind the castle are beaking in the sun, and over the dazzling Minch the seabirds are crying everlastingly. Peace reigns at Duntulm.

To reach Dunvegan from Duntulm you must travel south again by a road that is to me one long temptation to linger.

At Kilmuir Kirkyard—that wonderful view-point —who does not stop to visit the grave of Flora Macdonald? From Kilvaxter roadside you look down on the great meadows of Kilmuir where once lay the Loch of Columcille which was drained dry in 1824. In this moss you can see quite clearly the site of the old island monastery of the Columban monks—a tiny church on one islet, and a larger cashel on another, connected by a causeway. And,

if you know where to look, you will also catch
a glimpse of Monkstadt House to which Flora
Macdonald boldly led Prince Charlie when he was
dressed up as gaukie "Betty Burke." Then the
Dun of Skudiburgh, and from the road above the
beautiful Bay of Uig you look due west across
Loch Snizort to the rocky Ascrib Isles and the
Point of Vaternish, and due south to the line of
the purple Coolins.

If lingering were allowed I could tell a tale
of all these places ; and then go sauntering past
Earlish with its little crofts ; Kingsburgh with
another salute to Flora Macdonald ; the great bald
kirk of Snizort ; and so, by Skeabost, Lynedale,
Edinbain, and the Fairy Bridge to Dunvegan.
Only—I would be greatly tempted to travel once
more up the road past Stein to Trumpan, and tell
you the tragic story of Lady Grange, who lies
buried in the lonely kirkyard of Trumpan. Nor
could I hold back that other tale of the Battle of
the Spoiled Dykes down yonder by the green flats
at the head of Ardmore Bay.

I have long lost count of the times that I have
been at Dunvegan, and I am saddened now by the
thought that Norman, the twenty-third Chief of
Macleod, is dead.

I came first to Dunvegan in the long ago by sea,
when the distant glimpse of its grey walls seemed
the realisation of a lad's fondest dreams. Since
then, I have approached it from every airt, by land
and sea, and of all the great houses I have ever
seen, Dunvegan still holds my heart as the most
romantic Hall of Faerie. It is the only ancient

castle in Skye that is to-day inhabited by a family whose origin is lost in antiquity. When you cross the doorstep of Dunvegan, your one hand is on the balustrade of the present, and your other is groping in the mists of legendry.

The Dunvegan tradition has it that the first Leod of Harris was the son of Olaf the Black, King of Man. Over the front door of Dunvegan there is a stone bearing the arms of the sixteenth chief, and in this coat are the arms of the Isle of Man. Leod was the adopted heir of Paal Baalkeson, who was sheriff of Skye under the Norse Kings of Man. He owned Sleat, Trotternish, Waternish, and Snizort, and bequeathed all these lands to Leod, passing over his own natural son. Paal was killed in 1231, and with Paal Baalkeson Leod seems to have spent his early days at Duntulm, Dunscaith, and Castle Camus. Some time about 1220, Leod married a daughter of MacCrailt Armuinn, who was Lord of Dunvegan, and owned Duirinish, Bracadale, and Minginish. In the Gaelic MacCrailt became MacArailt, which means the son of Harold, and it is possible that the MacCrailts had been settled at Dunvegan from the end of the ninth century, when many Norsemen were driven away from their native land by Harold Haarfagre. The Armuinns were a kind of second order of nobility and ranked next to the Thanes. This marriage of Leod to MacCrailt's daughter brought Dunvegan and all its wide lands into Leod's family, and to-day Dunvegan is the castle of the twenty-third descendant in unbroken line.

The place was called the Dun of Began, doubtless

after one of MacCrailt's ancestors, and there is still a place in Iceland called Becanstadt. Moreover, at Trumpan kirkyard in Vaternish I have seen a tombstone with the name of *RACHEL M^CRAILD*—*d*. 1924. So the thirteenth century and the twentieth join hands at Dunvegan. The atmosphere of this castle in Skye is a thousand years old, and in the veins of the Chief who entertained his visitors so courteously there flowed the blood of MacCrailt Armuinn and the first of all the Leods.

I cannot here enlarge on the treasures of Dunvegan which have accumulated in the old keep for centuries. The Fairy Flag, which was given to Macleod by the elfin wife he married, as a magic mascot which he might wave three times in a moment of threatened danger, and which was indeed waved twice but never again. The Drinking Horn of Rory Mor, which each new chief had to drain of liquor to the dregs in one draught that he might prove his manhood. The beautiful Dunvegan Cup, which has the date 1493 carved on its rim, and a wooden bowl that is believed to date from the tenth century, once the property of Neil Glundubh, who was King of Ulster about 900. Here also you will see letters from Dr Samuel Johnson and Sir Walter Scott, both of whom were favoured guests at Dunvegan. Flora Macdonald's pin cushion; Prince Charlie's waistcoat and hair; a portrait of the wicked chief in black and red; another of Macleod, and still another of his lady—both by Sir Henry Raeburn, and the famous one of Dr Johnson by Sir Joshua Reynolds. The

LORD MACDONALD'S FOREST

MacCrimmon bagpipes are here also, and although I got the offer to put a tune on them, with a very proper reverence, I declined even to touch them.

Would that I could tell you some tales of Alastair Crotach, the eighth chief, and of Sir Rory Mor, the thirteenth; of the Fairy Room and its legends; of the Sea Gate and the bloody battles; of the desperate feuds and burnings between the Macleods and Macdonalds. Indeed, Skye was a wild world until the 'Forty-Five. I shall never forget passing from the pleasant drawing-room to the dungeon close by, along with the Chief, who lit a candle and let it down on a string through the opening in the stone floor to light the rock-hewn chamber below. From this chamber of horrors there is no possible exit. I can still see the kilted figure standing in the dim light saying with a smile on his face:

"It was down there that my ancestor put his first wife and starved her to death."

We then adjourned to the dining-room and saw the portrait of the Wicked Chief; one of his first wife whom he got rid of—a rather plain-looking lady; and another of the second wife—a distinctly good-looking lady. To dine here is to sit cheek by jowl with the tragedies of your own family history.

But my most romantic memory of Dunvegan is a picture of Norman, the twenty-third of his line, standing by the battlements of the ancient tower, in all the dignity of his tartan dress, with the eagle feathers of a chief set gaily in his bonnet. He was gazing into the eye of a June sunset, and at the

F

islands lying in the lap of the sea, and it seemed that he was looking away to Tir-nan-og, that Land of the Ever Young, where war no longer robs the brave of victory, and the happy Celts pursue the arts of peace.

IX

SCUIR NAN GILLEAN

THE PEAK OF THE YOUNG MEN

THE Coolins are the finest mountains in Britain. But be it far from a mere scrambler on the roof of Scotland to speak of rock climbing in Skye. That is for the experts alone. And yet, if in this magic world of mist and sunshine, islands and seas, one may speak of the hills of heaven, surely the heart and eyes of every mountain lover must instinctively turn to the Coolins !

There is a hardy little army of mountaineers, both old and young, who come year after year to Sligachan, that they may repeat old climbs and conquer new difficulties. For boon companions you will find no better on earth. I do not, however, write for them. Rather am I thinking now of the wayfaring man who comes to Skye for the first time with a natural desire to climb one of these ethereal peaks. Sooner or later he will find himself at Sligachan—that climbers' paradise—and then, all will depend on the weather whether his one precious day is to be a dismal failure or a blessed memory that will live with him to the end of life.

If the day be doubtful, this will happen to him which has happened to most of us. He will probably set out on an excursion up Bruach na Frithe, the easiest summit to reach from Sligachan, but a hill that has a most wonderful view. Not far from the Red Burn the drizzle will begin. The higher he ascends the burn the heavier the rain will come down. When he crosses the Bealach a' Mhaim, and makes up the slopes of Bruach na Frithe itself, the Skye deluge will be at its best. Yet, when he gains the ridge, the mist may lift for a moment, and right below him in the lower lights he will see the Glen Brittle river gleaming like silver on its way to the sea. But if the rain clouds have settled in, the sooner he retraces his steps the better. He may now be soaked to the skin. He will not need to pick his steps across the Red Burn. He will go right through it without any delicate manœuvres. Even if he sits down on a wet clump of heather to light a pipe, he may do so, for nothing can make him wetter. That is one of the blessings of Skye rain—it does away with a whole host of the politer anxieties.

But Skye is like a sweetheart that is always surprising us with her changing moods. Until you have thus been drenched and disappointed by wet weather among the Coolins, you will never know the bliss of being favoured with a heavenly day for your climb.

I can remember one such day.

We arrived at the Inn in the most brilliant weather. A clear shining day that was all the more wonderful because there had been heavy rain. Not a cloud or shred of mist rested on the splintered peaks, and the visibility was perfect.

We were a very jolly company of all ages and sizes. An English climber, his three boys, a tall Scots girl, and her elderly father in a kilt. Old John Mackenzie, who was waiting outside the Inn for the Professor, threw some sage advice at us with a bit of Gaelic humour in the passing. So with a hitch of the rucksack we set off up the old path. Glamaig smiled on us, and we remembered that a fleet-footed Indian gurkha once reached the top and returned to the bridge in fifty-five minutes. Little Marsco, which always looks like a Cardinal with his cap on, gave us his blessing. The blue Coolins were all about us, and the long light day was before us.

The route from Sligachan lies south over the moors. After crossing the Red Burn by the stepping stones near the old house, you top a low ridge and see a little loch lying to your left in Coire Riabhach. Then you go up a stone shoot into Coire nan Allt Geala. Finally, the south-east ridge is gained by scrambling up a long scree. After that you follow the ridge to the right, and it is now only a matter of time until you reach the summit. When you are climbing the last hundred feet or so, hands as well as feet come into play. But for those who cannot manage the Pinnacles of Scuir nan Gillean, this is the safe way, which none need despise who would look upon one of the most glorious views in the world.

Scrambling up rocks, like those on the top of the Coolins, entails a certain amount of knee work. So, when the elderly man in the kilt joined the others on the summit, youth made some rude remarks about a pair of ruddy knees.

The view held us spellbound. Here was Skye at its best. Hot rocks on the high tops. Not a breath of wind. An almost cloudless sky. The whole of the western seaboard, the outer Hebrides, the inner isles, and Eilean a Cheo itself spread out below us like a map. Looking down into Lota Coire we saw nothing but desolation. But from Harris to Ross, on sea and land, it was an elusive world of beauty.

Wherever youth is, age gets little chance to dream of the sublime, and we were soon brought down to the ridiculous. For the three boys proceeded to empty their pockets. One had an air pistol and began to shoot at nothing. Another had a whistle which split the silence in two. The third had actually carried up a tiny brass cannon, which he had moulded with his own hands, and a supply of gunpowder. He loaded the cannon twice with powder and shot, and fired at Kyleakin lighthouse. Surely a historic moment. For no cannon had ever been fired from the top of Scuir nan Gillean before. Being at a well-known Quaker school in England he was punished for making this weapon of war. There being no loose pebbles on the top, and remembering a well-known rule of mountaineering, that no stone should ever be sent down on those who are below you on a hill, it seemed useless to bring out the catapult.

And it was just as well. For when the mock bombardment was over, we were startled by seeing the face of a young man, who had come up on another climb, looking at us over the edge of the summit rocks. Very hot and dishevelled, he came slowly on to the ledge, followed by another climber. They were members of the English Rucksack Club, and immediately found a fellow-member in the father of the three boys. One of them had sadly torn clothes, both knees of his trousers being ruined, and another part of the same garment almost entirely gone.

"What do you think of these black gabbro rocks? Fine for climbing, are they not?" remarked the man in the kilt, with a smile, as he rubbed some blood from his knees.

"Yes," replied the young Englishman rather slowly, for he was thinking of that part of his garment which he could not see, "one week in the Coolins does more damage than two seasons in Cumberland."

We were just settling in for a talk when once more a head appeared above the rocks from the other side.

"Hullo!"

And a member of the Junior Scottish Mountaineering Club thrust his tousled head upon us. A second followed him, and when the rope was taken off the three Scotsmen recognised each other.

So we were a merry party of ten crowded on the top. A feast of coffee and fat things followed. Cameras snapped. Then we separated, and took our own ways down to Sligachan.

The day was done. But the memory of it will linger for ever to cheer many a wintry hour in the far-off city when, amid the rush of ordinary affairs, we lift our eyes above the crowded pavements and behold from the peak of Scuir nan Gillean the islands of the west lying in that azure sea.

Late that night we were fifteen miles from Sligachan. But when we looked to the west the Coolins stood out against the pale green sky like purple mountains in a dream. One crimson cloud still hung above the hills, and the hush of heaven lay over the sea.

X

THE BRAVE SONS OF SKYE

AN INCOMPARABLE RECORD

THE Celt's love of home has always been pain-drenched by his incurable lust for wandering beyond it. His pride of life is contemptuous of either gold or gear. Gallant beyond all others when he looks into the eyes of death, this has been his battle-cry throughout the ages:

> Danger no refuge holds, and war no peace.

The finest lovers and the fiercest fighters in the world, whose souls have ever been aflame with the high gest, and whose songs are full of the insatiable love which is always tinged with sorrow, through all the adventures of the immemorial years, O Highland hearts, we salute you still!

Far be it from me to set the sons of one Hebrid isle against the sons of another. But it is my privilege now to relate the story of the Brave Sons of Skye, remembering the incomparable record that was compiled over thirty years ago, under that stirring title, by one of themselves, from authentic military sources, with one hundred portraits of those gallant Skyemen.

The Clan system was completely broken down after the 'Forty-Five. But nothing could kill the fighting spirit of the Celt. So, in a remarkably short time after the stramash of Culloden, a wise Government encouraged the enlistment of thousands of Highlanders whose fathers had fought for Prince Charlie, and thus the Highland regiments were raised for service in the foreign wars.

Here is proof of this wise policy.

William Pitt, afterwards Earl of Chatham, once used these words in addressing the House of Commons :

" I have sought for merit wherever it could be found. It is my boast that I was the first Minister who looked for it, and found it in the mountains of the North. I called it forth, and drew into your service a hardy and intrepid race of men ; men who, when left by your jealousy, became a prey to the artifices of your enemies, and had gone nigh to have overturned the State in the war before last. But these men in the last war were brought to combat on your side; they served with fidelity, as they fought with valour, in every quarter of the globe."

And what response did the Brave Sons of Skye make to this appeal of the great Minister of State ?

Only about fifty years after the defeat of the Highlanders at Culloden, and after the shameful treatment of the fugitives by Cumberland, followed by the Disarming Act of 12th August 1746, which made not only the carrying of all weapons illegal, but suppressed the wearing of every kind of Highland dress, the Highlanders began to enlist in the

British Army. We are told by a former Adjutant-General of the Forces that in the forty years which preceded the crowning of Queen Victoria (1797-1837) the Island of Skye alone provided the armies of Great Britain with 21 lieutenant-generals and major-generals, 45 lieutenant-colonels, 600 majors, captains and subalterns, 10,000 private soldiers, 120 pipers, 4 governors of British Colonies, 1 Governor-General of India, and 1 adjutant-general of the British Army. More remarkable still, we have it on the same authority that 1600 Skyemen fought in the ranks at Waterloo.

So Skye gave to the Army 666 officers and 10,000 private soldiers, with 120 pipers, within a space of forty years.

It was while Alexander Smith was staying with M'Ian of Ord, that fine old army veteran, that he heard great tales of the Brave Sons of Skye, and so we read in " A Summer in Skye " this remarkable tribute to the men of " An t'Eilean " :

" Love of wandering and pride in military life have been characteristic of all the old families. . . . They have had representatives in every Peninsular and Indian battle-field. . . . Of the miniatures kept in every family more than one-half are soldiers. . . . The tartans waved through the smoke of every British battle, and there were no such desperate bayonet charges as those which rushed to the yell of the bagpipe. At the close of the last and the beginning of the present century, half the farms in Skye were rented by half-pay officers. The Army List was to the island what the Post Office Directory is to London."

What a difference has come over Skye to-day:

O hearts to the hills of old memory true!
In the land of your love there are mourners for you,
As they wander by peopleless lochside and glen,
Where the red deer are feeding o'er homesteads of men.

PRINCIPAL SHAIRP.

To write an account of all these Brave Sons of Skye would be an impossible task. So I shall take but one example of a Highland family to show how these remarkable men and women served their King and country at home, and crossed the seas as emigrants to found whole colonies of Gaelic-speaking folks, fighting there when necessary as soldiers of the King, and all the while yearning for the misty island which they could never forget.

There is a remote place on the north-east shores of Trotternish to which my thoughts often fly. It is the historic little estate of Flodigarry. This was one of the seats of the famous family of Macdonald of Kingsburgh, and the tale of Flora Macdonald is one of the romances of the world. Flora married Allan the VIIth of Kingsburgh and Flodigarry, and the story of that family is typical of the Brave Sons of Skye.

Allan's early life was spent at Kingsburgh. His father, Alexander VI. of Kingsburgh, was chamberlain to his Chief, and in those days much of the rent was paid in kind—that is, in cattle, sheep, etc. The cattle were collected from every part of the Macdonald estates by drovers, who brought them to Kyle Rhea. There the beasts were taken across the ferry or swam the strait, and were driven all the way south to Falkirk Tryst. Allan, who had all the responsibility for the sale of the cattle, was known locally as " Ailean na mile mart," or " Allan of the Thousand Cattle." About the year 1734 his father, Alexander, bought the estate of Flodigarry from John Martin, and handed over the place to Allan, who took up his residence there.

Allan Macdonald was a handsome man with a powerful physique and a great reputation for wrestling. Early in 1745 Flora Macdonald came back from Edinburgh with Lady Margaret Macdonald to Monkstadt House, the principal seat of the Macdonalds in Skye. Flodigarry is about six miles across the hills as the crow flies, and Allan must often have crossed the island to cultivate the acquaintance of Flora. But, like all true lovers, they had to wait a long time and pass through much anxiety before they pledged their troth. In June of the same year Flora returned to her father's house at Milton in South Uist.

Then came the stirring events of the 'Forty-Five, the march south to Edinburgh and far-off Derby, the retreat to the Highlands, and the flight of Prince Charlie after Culloden in 1746.

Who can ever forget the story of Prince Charlie and his voyage from Uist to Skye in the boat with Flora Macdonald, who saved him from his pursuers by taking the Prince across the Minch as her female attendant under the name of " Betty Burke " ? The story is too well known to need repetition.

Flora was later taken to London on H.M.S. *Furious* and detained there. No Jacobite ladies were ever brought to trial. They were only " detained " privately in Messengers' Houses—that is, selected prisoners lived in the private premises of Court officials, and their treatment largely depended on the length of their purses. The captivity, however, was not severe, and the Messenger—one Dick—with whom Flora was detained kept in his easy custody many distinguished Jacobites like herself and Æneas Macdonald, the banker. Indeed, Æneas tells us that while in Dick's House he was taken away to Newgate because he was " concerting a jaunt to Windsor with Flora Macdonald."

Flora was not set at liberty till the end of 1747. The reunion of the lovers took place at Monkstadt House, where Sir Alexander and Lady Macdonald gave a ball in honour of Flora's return. Allan's father had also been confined for the best part of a year in Edinburgh Castle, and during his absence his estate had been greatly impoverished. Here is a notice of the wedding in the *Scots Magazine* : " November 6th, at Armadale, Sleat, Allan Macdonald, eldest son of Alexander Macdonald of Kingsburgh, married to Miss Flora Macdonald, daughter of Ranald Macdonald of Milton, deceased. This is the young lady who aided the escape of the Young Chevalier."

All their children were born at Flodigarry—five sons and two daughters. Needless to say, the eldest son was called Charles, after the Prince.

Old Kingsburgh died in 1772, aged 83, and Allan, after twenty years of happy life at Flodigarry, removed to Kingsburgh. In July of that year Pennant visited him, and has recorded that Kingsburgh gave him, on parting, three gifts—an urn filled with ashes; a lucky Druidical glass bead, with serpents marked on it; and a Roman coin, a *Denarius* of the Emperor Trajan, which was found near Loch Greshornish. Pennant suggests that it may have been picked up by an island soldier when skirmishing with the Romans farther south.

In the autumn of 1773 Samuel Johnson and Boswell paid Kingsburgh a visit, and Boswell has left us an inimitable picture of Allan Macdonald:

" Kingsburgh was completely the picture of a gallant Highlander. . . . He had his tartan plaid thrown about him, a large blue bonnet with a knot of blue riband like a cockade, a brown short coat of a kind of duffel, a tartan waistcoat with gold buttons and gold button-holes, a bluish philibeg and tartan hose. He had jet black hair tied behind, and was a large, stately man, with a steady, sensible countenance."

Of Kingsburgh's Lady, Johnson writes these words, which are now carved on Flora Macdonald's monument at Kilmuir: " Flora Macdonald, a name that will be mentioned in history, and if courage and fidelity be virtues, mentioned with honour."

Both Johnson and Boswell slept in the Prince's room at Kingsburgh, and Johnson occupied the bed which the Prince had slept in. They talked that night of the unique experience, and in the morning Boswell found on the bedroom table a slip of paper on which Johnson had written these words:

> Quantum cedat virtutibus aurum.
> (With virtue weighed, what trash is gold !)

Doubtless Johnson was thinking of the utter loyalty of the Highlanders to their Prince, for not one of them was tempted by the £30,000 reward which the Government offered for news of his whereabouts.

But Boswell remarks that Kingsburgh was embarrassed in his affairs, and was even then thinking of emigration. So the next year, in August 1774, Allan Macdonald and Flora, his wife, with all their family, except Charles and John, sailed in the ship *Baliol* from Campbeltown to Wilmington, on the Cape Fear River, in North Carolina.

What an adventure emigration was in those days! The *Baliol* was attacked by a French privateer, and a fierce fight took place. Flora Macdonald refused to go below when the firing began, but remained on deck where all her family were engaged in battle. During the mêlée her arm was broken, and a young clansman, Kenneth Macdonald, who had studied surgery in Glasgow, set her arm and bound it up.

Their fellow-countrymen gave the Macdonalds a great welcome to Carolina, where Flora's fame had preceded her. At Cross Creek, a hundred miles further up the river, there was a Highland settlement. But they moved on to Cameron's Hill, and, finally, Allan bought land in an outlying part of the colony, and called his new home Killiegray.

The Highlanders arrived just about the time the Home Government and the American colonists were beginning to quarrel, and in 1775 the crisis came. After a skirmish at Lexington in April the Battle of Bunker Hill was fought on 17th June.

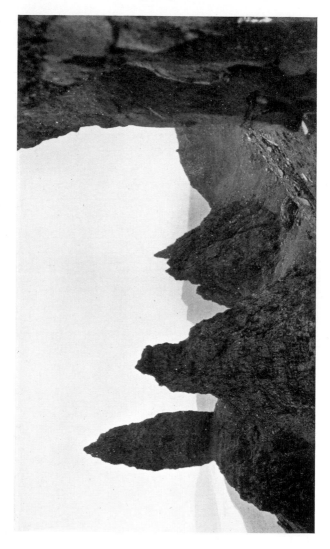

THE STORR ROCKS

So in Carolina, as long before in Skye, the Celts heard the old call to arms :

> Danger no refuge holds, and war no peace.

A regiment of Highland emigrants was at once raised, and the whole corps was dressed and accoutred in the manner of the Black Watch, under the name of the Royal Highland Emigrants. Allan Macdonald became a Captain, and his son Alexander was appointed a Lieutenant. Then followed fierce fighting and years of service. Both were taken prisoners, but were released on exchange. They saw service at New York, Halifax, the Spanish River, Cape Breton, and cruising about the Canadian coast. Then they remained in Nova Scotia until peace was declared in 1783, when Allan and the other Captains of the 2nd Battalion received from the Government a grant of 5000 acres of land near Halifax.

But the old yearning for home overcame Flora and her daughters, and long before the war was over they returned to Skye, in the year 1779. Allan saw the fighting through, and then, like many another Highland gentleman, he trekked home in 1784 to take up the old holding at Kingsburgh. For six happy years he and his wife lived there, until Flora died in 1790. Allan lingered till 1792, when he also passed over. Such is the story of an illustrious Highland family.

To-day Allan and Flora lie side by side in the old Kirkyard of Kilmuir. I saw a new-made grave close by, and farther off I took a drawing of an old grey effigy of a knight in armour. For love is old yet ever new, and the sob at the heart is the same in all generations. The summer day seemed almost hurting in its beauty as I sat among the graves and dreamed. Flora's Monument towered above the humbler headstones, and looked right out to the Hebrid Isles, which lay on the rim of the west like islands of the blest on a sea of glass.

> For the stillness they feel o'er the wilderness spread
> Is not Nature's own silence, but that of the dead ;
> E'en the lone piping plover and small corrie burn
> Seem sighing for those that will never return.
>
> PRINCIPAL SHAIRP.

ROSS

XI

SUDDEN SUMMER

A SUNBURST AT GAIRLOCH

I can always write best about heat when I am shivering with cold. For imagination is not a lying jade, as so many people seem to think. It is only that power by which man can recall, visualise, re-create, and even feel some perfectly true experience which may be long past. Do we not all enjoy reading articles about the sunshine and the flowers in dark December ? So I have always maintained that we never get the full benefit of our summer holidays until midwinter.

On these bitter days of February, when, like exiles of hope, we have all been living in Arctic conditions, it is not only good but natural to make an attempt to recapture the burning heat of the sun. A Scots summer can be bitterly disappointing, and we sometimes sigh in July for the sun. It was, therefore, in some such mood of chilled resignation that we prepared to go North last August, muttering to ourselves something about " the bitter East, the misty summer."

And then—the miracle happened !

That very morning the warm spell leaped upon

us. The bell heather flamed like fire above Pit-
lochry. The moors of Drumouchter lay shimmer-
ing in the heat. From the heights of Drumossie
we feasted our eyes on the heartsome panorama of
Inverness lying in the lap of beauty, surrounded by
the fertile fields that fringe the firth, with the mas-
sive ramparts of Wyvis beyond, and the dim blue
mountains of Ross far away. The farther we went
—by Achnasheen, Kinlochewe, Loch Maree, and
Kerrysdale—the more heat and beauty we found,
until we came to the shores of the Western sea.
It was not the least of our mercies that our windows
looked across the sea to Skye. Truly, the road that
leads north, with a slant westward to the Minch, is
the best road of all.

It was St Francis who first praised God for our
blessed brother the Sun. Here, day after day, the
sun poured down upon us a heavenly benediction
of heat. We could not escape from the fiery fur-
nace. Sitting on the heather, on the sands, in a
boat at sea, we were soon burned brick-red. But
the very fierceness of the sun drew forth all the most
delicious scents of nature—a resinous whiff from the
pine trees when the warm days were windless ; the
refreshing tang of bog myrtle in the wet places of
the moor ; the fragrance of honey in the air when
we plunged knee-deep through the heather. To
lie on the back and dream on such a bed of purple
was to feel the old worries slipping from the soul.
Then came summer sleep to the drone of bees.

To all this peace was added a beauty which no
pen can ever describe. The sea rippled across the
golden sands. There was a constant gluck of little

waves where the rocks cast a sheltering arm round the bay. The shallows were iridescent with every shade of amber, amethyst, and green. The majestic Ross-shire hills—Boshven and Alligan—looked ethereal and unreal in the heat haze, and the long elusive line of Skye lay like a cloud on the rim of the horizon. And when the burning day was done the sun went down behind the little moors of Strath, not with the flaming glories which so often make the Western sky tragic after a day of storm, but with a holy quietness that filled the heart like an evening benediction. Then the blue-dusk sky, with a star or two, and the cool oblivion of sleep.

When the days became insufferably warm we crawled along to the sands. The glistering beaches, someone has called them. Here was sea-water that was cool enough to be refreshing, yet warm enough to give pleasure. Down in the holy hollow of the *Leabaidh*—that green bed in the dunes where for generations the good folks of Gairloch sat at the white tables and remembered Christ—not a breath of wind tempered the heat. But beyond the dunes lie the sands, and where the golden circle ends the rocks make a paradise for those who swim.

Who can describe this most blessed of all summer delights? Standing erect in the blazing sun, arms raised for the adventurous plunge, a rush of liquid music in the ears as the green depths are explored, and sheer buoyancy brings us up to the sunlight again.

> Cold throbs of life, light as the bubbles surging
> From the swift encircling hand ;

On throat and hair the quivering ice-stars breaking
   Like foam of silver wine ;
Waves of exulting thought in sense awaking
   Glamour of youth divine.

Welcome the breathless marge ! the sunlight burning
   From new caressing skies !
A luxury of rest in warmth returning,
   Laughter for clearer eyes.

G. WINTHROP YOUNG.

Surrounded by youth and its care-free laughter in this place of mermaid pleasures, it was easy to recapture the heart of a boy, and to forget that there was any such thing as care in all the happy world.

One day I sat high up amid the waste of bogs and moors that lie above North Erradale. Here the silence of death seemed to reign. From this point the view is wide and wonderful. The mountains of Torridon rise to the south, the great hunch of Liagach, and the mighty tops of Ben Eighe. I could see the loom of the Applecross hills above the long flat line of moors that run out to Red Point. Rona, Raasay, and Northern Skye floated in the misty silence. The heat was too great to make it possible to see the Outer Isles. One boat lay becalmed on the shining sea. Longay, like a bottle-nosed whale, rose from the water in the near distance. There was no sign of life, no sound, only an occasional whisper of mysterious airs about the ears. All nature seemed to have swooned, and the silence rang across the moors like a little bell of God to recall a wanderer to a sense of eternal things. Then a solitary whaup cried eerily, as if seeking its lost mate. Far away in a croft at Erradale a cock crowed. The whole landscape seemed to cry out of the dead old days when this world of bogs and mountains was one vast forest, with a race of Celtic heroes fighting blood feuds among the trees, and living on the bare bones of existence. At any moment ghosts of the past might peer at you from behind the hummocks and lichen-covered boulders. That very bunch of red-pine roots at my feet, which has been gathered from the peat haggs, is part of the primeval forest through which the wild boars routed after their food. Here is the blessing of the separate. For, as the old blind gangrel said to me long ago:

" You can never win close to things till you climb high, all your lone, where there is nobody else to break the thrum."

It was a long, hot descent to the shore at Carn Dearg, in the blazing sun. But a plunge into the cool green sea, the pine roots burning brightly on the hot rocks, and there was peace and plenty by the edge of the whispering tide.

Even on the water it was hard to find coolness. For the glassy sea threw back the heat as from the surface of a burnished mirror. The old boat chug-chugged its way across the mouth of the Kerry river, past the bay of Shieldaig, between the isle of Horrisdale and the tiny land-locked village of Badachro, and right out to the tilted rocks of Opinan. We found a delicious well on the shore, with an old causeway leading to it, and here the blue reek was soon rising into the still air.

There is a flat rock that shelves into the deep

water near Shieldaig Bay. It is called the *Leac-nan-saighead*, or the Slab of the Arrow. And this is the tale you will hear at the *ceilidh*.

As far back as 1480 a commission of fire and sword was granted by the king to Hector Roy Mackenzie to exterminate the Gairloch Macleods. Be very sure the Macleods bitterly resented being expelled from Gairloch, for they never were a small-souled clan. So they sat for a time in the hall at Dunvegan brooding revenge. It was then that Fair-haired Sarah, an old Skye *cailleach* with the sight, urged them on to go back and gain their own again on the shores of Ross. Up they sprang and crowded into the black birlinn. It was the dusk of day when they sailed into Gairloch, and night when they landed on little Fraoch Eilean. There they hid themselves till morning.

But Donald and Ian Odhar, the famous Macrae archers, had spied on their coming. So they stole round the shores in the deep of night to *Leac-nan-saighead*. The flat Slab of the Arrow overlooks Fraoch Eilean. Standing on the step of this rock, yet concealed from any one watching from the island, the Macrae archers began to shoot at dawn. Some of the Macleods were killed before they found out the spot from which the deadly arrows came. Then their comrades began to return the fire. But their arrows were only splintered on the *Leac-nan-saighead*. At last one of the Macleods, in exasperation, climbed the mast of the birlinn, to get a better view of the enemy. Ian Odhar saw him, fitted an arrow to his string, and nailed the Macleod to the mast.

" You have sent a pin through his broth ! " said Donald Odhar.

So the slaughter went on until only two Macleods escaped in the birlinn. For the rest, trenches were dug on the island, and to-day you can see the green howes.

Sad tales, with blood in every one of them.

Now, alas, the sun has gone. The weather is broken. The clouds are down on Skye. There is a tang of autumn in the air. A robin is singing his plaintive song in the woods at Flowerdale—that song which always means good-bye to summer. The night closes in with a steady downpour of rain, and the wind moans eerily about the chimneys on the Hill of Treasure. But we have had our sunburst, and are content to rest our souls in memory.

XII

GLEN TORRIDON

AND THE ROAD TO DIABAIG

IT is useless to ask what is the finest glen in Scotland. Glens are like people. Each has its own character, its own scenery, its own beauty, and its own history.

So with Glen Torridon. No other glen could be mistaken for it. But it is something of an adventure to describe a region whose very road lies along the oldest floor in the world. Wild, desolate, remote—it is all that, this unpeopled glen where an occasional rickle of stones cries out of a race that is now no more. When you have used up all the adjectives, there is something more about Torridon —an indescribable something which grips you with a sense of the unutterable.

The glen, moreover, has a lonely outgait to the Western sea. At first sight Loch Torridon seems to be nothing but a land-locked lake, with the blue line of the Skye hills above its rather low shores. But when you look down from the hills above Alligan and Diabaig, Torridon is a mountain-encircled arm of the sea, eleven miles long from the little Ploc at its head to Rhu na Fearn at its mouth, with three distinct reaches—the Upper Loch, Loch Shieldaig, and Loch Torridon proper —slanting northwards to the Minch.

The bounds of Torridon can be described in one bald paragraph. The loch is exactly the same length as the glen, which is dominated by two great mountains—Ben Eighe and Liagach. If you have travelled from Achnasheen down Glen Dochartie, you will find the road to Torridon striking off to the left just beyond Kinlochewe, and all the way to the sea it never rises above 400 feet. About four miles along this desolate road lies lovely Loch Clair on the south side, and you get a glimpse of Coulin Lodge among the trees, with Scuir Dubh and the mountains of Coulin forest behind. These are the bounds of Glen Torridon.

But who can describe this silent glen, which is one of the oldest ante-chambers of the world! Travelling on this roadway, you are passing over one of the first foundations of the earth. For these great mountains of Torridon sandstone rise directly from a primeval bed of gneiss.

Not many weeks ago, when passing through Torridon, I tried to explain to a Highlander the age of his own glen, for his oft-repeated questions demanded an answer :

" How did the like o' that big rock get there ? "

" How were the like o' these cliffs made ? "

" If the ice made these scratches, why are there no frosts and ice the like o' that now ? "

So I pointed to Liagach. For I know no mountain in Scotland which gives us a more instant sense of the age of the earth. It stands on the oldest rock in the world. It rises steeply from the roadway. Its walls represent unimaginable ages of creation. Yet, from its roots in the primeval gneiss, up these terrific sandstone terraces to the very top of its white quartzite cap, the eye can take in at a glance the whole three thousand feet of age-less masonry.

> Liagach rising sheer
>   From river-bed up to the sky,
> Grey courses of masonry tier on tier,
>   And pinnacles splintered on high.
>
> Splintered, contorted, and riven,
>   As though, from the topmost crown
> Some giant plougher his share had driven
>   In a hundred furrows sheer down.
>
> PRINCIPAL SHAIRP.

The sandstone cliffs tell us of God's first great seas, and of the æons of time which must have elapsed ere these grim precipices were slowly deposited, grain by grain, and shelf by shelf. How often, after that, must the earth have been rocked to its primal founds, with mighty upheavals that cracked and twisted and crumpled the strata, sending tremendous overthrusts of one rocky world on to the top of another! Then came the age of ice, when this unpeopled land was slowly ground down, and carved out into glens and corries. The waters of the melted ice gradually receded, and now these smooth and deeply scratched surfaces remain to this day on the level places of Maree and Torridon. Truly, Liagach must have taken an eternity to build. And yet that was only a little bit of time!

Take your stand on any viewpoint of these hills, and if the visibility is good, your eye, ranging over Ross and Sutherland, will pick up a great many mountains of similar form which pierce the sky like pyramids — Quinag, Canisp, Suilven, Cul Mhor, the Coygach hills, the Teallach mountains in the Dundonnell forest, Slioch, Ben Eighe, Liagach—all children of the same primeval family, standing like silent sentinels of time which have withstood the desolations of incalculable ages.

And what colour the Almighty Artist has lavished on these ancient hills !

The blues and greys of the original gneiss, the warm hues of the sandstone terraces, the gleam of the white quartzite caps. I have seen them steeped in the light of the setting sun, the lower rocks all blue with shadows in the mystic twilight of the glen, the red cliffs glowing in the level rays, and the cones of snow lifting their heads majestically to catch the last beams of the dying day.

> Benyea, magnificent alp,
>   Blanched bare and bald and white,
> His forehead like old sea eagle's scalp,
>   Seen athwart the sunset light !

To view these Torridon mountains in the silence of a summer night—from a boat on Loch Maree, from the Bridge of Grudie, from the shores of Loch Clair, or from some point in Glen Torridon itself —is to be overawed with a sense of the wonder of the world and the age of the earth. For these are the

> Regions consecrate to oldest time.

On the south side of Glen Torridon lies the Corrie of a Hundred Hills. It is so-called because of a vast number of rounded, heather- and grass-covered hillocks which lie there. These little moraine dumps, which geologists call *roches moutonnées*, or rocky sheepbacks, are also a legacy from the melted ice of the glaciers.

Very often in a glen, or on the level floor of a Highland valley, you will see these rounded mounds standing there, bare and green, or covered with trees. The Celts call them Shians, or Fairy Knolls. If the wee folks still hold their revels in the remote places of the north, calling strangely from below and making compelling music which no mortal can with safety listen to, then the Corrie of a Hundred Hills must be a weird place for wandering, either in a summer gloaming, or in the mirk of a winter forenight.

Come to Torridon any way you please, you will come to the end of a lonesome world. There is here no through-going road. A motorist cannot take Torridon in the passing. It is a bit of un-spoiled mountain solitude. The road ends at the gates of Torridon House. At the very head of the loch there is a fine example of a *cairidh*, set across the tidal way from shore to shore. Here, when the tide recedes, the fish are imprisoned. Between the village and the lodge gate a slab of stone stands by the roadside to keep green the memory of a beloved laird. The inscription is as follows :

" This stone was erected in 1912 by Ann, widow of Duncan Darroch, of Gourock and Torridon, in memory of the devotion and affection shown by one hundred men on the estate of Torridon, who, at their own request, carried his body from the house here on its way to interment in the family burial place at Gourock."

Would that every proprietor in the Highlands to-day knew his people and was loved by them like that !

> See that thou kindly use them, O man !
>   To whom God giveth
> Stewardship over them in thy short span,
>   Not for thy pleasure !
> Woe be to them who choose for a clan
>   Four-footed people !
>
> ALEX. NICOLSON.

By the goodwill of all concerned, the old right-of-way has just been restored from the lodge gate along the shore to the isolated village of Alligan. How much this means to the dwellers in Upper and Lower Alligan will be well understood when I describe the alternative road which leads over the hills for seven miles to Diabaig.

It is one of the wildest and most soul-satisfying hill roads I know, rising and falling about 1000 feet in a few miles, with some sensational gradients, a bad surface, hairpin bends to suit the taste of a trick rider, no passing places to speak of, and a hill as bad at the end as at the beginning. The road to Diabaig is a hill walker's ideal track. But it was my good fortune to drive over it in a little four-seater, with a lady at the wheel whose nerve is just as fine as her driving ability.

Near the top of the worst hill I was quite prepared to jump. Coming down this same hill on the return journey you have a clean view of the sea, 800 feet below the bottom of the road, but, mercifully, there is a hairpin bend just there, so you go round and not over. On the top level, where the road runs through the wild Bealach na Gaoithe, or the Windy Gowl, there are wonderful views from the shore of a little hill loch. Then the road once more takes a nasty dive for half a mile down a stony surface, with a bankless drop of several hundred feet to a solitary sheet of fresh water—Loch Diabaig Airde. A mile or so of easy going along the shores of this loch and we once more topped the rise which is above Loch Diabaig itself, where there is another truly testing hill down to the village on the seashore.

The return journey—always a thought—was just as exhilarating. But to those who would drive to Diabaig let me say three things—pray that your flight be not in bad weather, else the road will be like the bed of a stream ; that you have not to turn back, because you cannot ; and that you meet no other car either on the breast or the back of the bad hills, for then, like the two goats on the plank bridge, you must either go back or go over.

We stopped at a turning-place above Diabaig, and lit a fire for lunch. A stalker who had heard of our coming walked for an hour before he found us there. Here time and distance are as nothing. There on the heather, by the remains of the fire, we held one of the finest of *ceilidhs*.

There are days which are so heavenly that to win their glories all risks are justifiable. The whole world of Torridon lay about us—the great solitudes of Ben Alligan ; the summer sea flashing in the sun right over to the shores of Rona, Raasay, and

BEINN EIGHE FROM LOCH CLAIR

Skye ; the Applecross mountains across the loch ;
Shieldaig tucked away on its own loch, where the
road goes up the glen and over the hills to Kishorn ;
Loch Damph worming its way into the forest.
The peace of the day fell on us like a benediction
as we feasted our eyes on the far horizons, recognis-
ing the bens and glens and islands as only those can
who have loved them for a lifetime. We heard
some old-time tales of the passes through these
hills, and of the dool of those who long ago had
fought their battles there. But memory only re-
calls the peace, the beauty, and the happiness of
that day

> —the mountain Sabbath that ever more
> a sanctuary here doth keep.

H

XIII

THE OLD ROAD TO THE TIGH DIGE

OR THE ART OF WALKING SLOW

THIRTY-FIVE miles in one day is certainly good walking, and the first time I tramped this Kerrysdale road we kept up a speed of four miles an hour. But we were young then, and there were one or two things we did not know. One of them was, that slow-going is not always unheroic.

In this age of hurry, when most of us spend our time rushing about the world from one place to another, and an absent-minded pedestrian is not safe on a high road, we are beginning to realise that there is a great deal more than luck in leisure. That is why the old by-paths in the country are coming back to their own, where the contemplative man can walk in peace, and the poor soul who has been run off his feet in a city can look, and loiter, and listen to his heart's content.

You strike the old road as you cross the hills from Loch Maree to Gairloch. It begins at the Red Stable, on the shores of little Loch Bad na Scalaig, and wanders for miles among the moors, until it drops down opposite the old Tigh Dige at Flowerdale.

A derelict woodman's shack stands near the point where the track leaves the Kerrysdale road. A forsaken dwelling always fires the imagination. As we pass in at the open door one or two sheep scamper out and rush along the tiny veranda. When all the woods were waving in the wind up here this must have been a fine forester's shanty. But now! The great double stove in the main apartment is a rusted ruin : the paper is hanging from the walls ; a bunch of holly all withered and dry hangs from the roof, a pathetic relic of the last Christmas carousal. The whole place smells of decay. So we pass out and look round rather sadly on that which is now a common sight in the Highlands— a whole hill-side cleared of timber, with no sign of new woods taking the place of the old.

The road, which is covered in places with fine old turf, has been well built, as the ancient stone foundations at the corners show. The blessedness of an old road is, that it always leads you into a sanctuary of solitude. Up here there are no sounds but the sough of wandering winds, the whisper of little streams, and the drone of an industrious bee as it flits from one heather tuft to another. Gorgeous dragon-flies dart across the path ; butterflies flutter above the heather ; great purple-headed beetles rush about among the grasses on nimble legs ; little stick insects alight on the rocks, like tiny bits of bark, and rest themselves with that perfect mimicry for which Mother Nature is proverbial ; a big grasshopper with green armoured thorax, goggle eyes, and a most comical mouth, suns itself on a stone, its mighty legs cocked up like the cantilevers of a bridge. You have only to sit down by the old road, and look largely at Nature with your own eyes, or with a minuter vision through a pocket microscope, to see all that and a great deal more.

Then the track descends through a narrow little gorge, with a tiny stream flowing by the side of the green road, which is made beautiful here by a few birch trees. The music of that running water would soothe the soul of the most anxious. To wander thus in such a world, alert yet unhasting, is the only way to win the blessing of the loiterer. The far-off hoot of a motor reminds me of the words of one who himself has been an exquisite exponent of the refinements of loitering :

> Of speed, the savour and the sting,
>   None but the weak deride :
> But, ah, the joy of lingering
>   About the countryside !
> The swiftest wheel, the conquering run,
>   We count no privilege
> Beside acquiring, in the sun,
>   The secret of the hedge.
>
> E. V. Lucas.

There speaks the wise wanderer who does not despise speed when it is necessary, but who knows also the true value of leisure. A rhapsody of sauntering, a gloria of ease ; the delicate and gentle art of never getting there—these are some of the word poems of this most refined of loiterers who has given a whole generation the benefit of what his own quiet eyes have seen.

The pathway now opens out along the mountain

SLIOCH FROM GRUDIE

side, with wide views across Shieldaig forest, and one heartsome glimpse of the blue sea. At this point the road runs over a bit of flat glacier-worn rock. Another little shelving rock rises from the side of the path, with a heather bank above. Here is the obvious place for the midday meal. A fire is soon blazing against the upright rock. The reek rises against the grey bluff, and so disperses itself as to be invisible to the eye of a watcher. It is sheer luxury to lie in the heat, and do nothing but look and listen. What first-hand pleasures are here! The generous sunshine, the wide views of moors and mountains, midday peace, the husheen of invisible waters, two tramps who know what not to say, a simple meal, and a whiff of fragrant coffee. Add to this natural pleasure-house of God, the purple heather all honey-scented, the russet hues of birch and braken, the dull gold of fading mosses, and the glory is manifold.

After this the road swings round a corner and descends into a green hollow, where great trees stand on the old turf meadows. Nestling among the trees is a clachan of thatched houses, with one white-washed cottage. One of the trees by the roadside is a very old larch, with mighty arms that reach out and upwards, as is the habit of ancient larches. Looking at this majestic tree, one naturally thinks of the huge larches at Meggernie Castle, Monzie Castle, and Dunkeld House, for these were among the first larches to be planted in this country.

Sitting in this green glade, under the immemorial trees, a man of vision might dream through the livelong day, calling to mind tales of old-time travellers, or cavalcades of Highland retainers following the laird and his lady on their fine little garrons, with little children strapped into creels, as they all make their way down to the old Tigh Dige, which was the chief's dwelling-place.

To hurry here would be sacrilege. To leave the glade and climb the next stage of the journey, past a little forest of pines and birches, takes but a few minutes. But a great beech tree at the top of the rise offers another delightful temptation, for there are good temptations as well as bad in this alluring world. And the heat is an immediate excuse. What welcome shade these mighty beech branches afford ! The wind sends a refreshing swish through the myriad leaves, and, as we listen, a phrase of Robert Louis Stevenson lingers in the memory :

Green days in forests.

No matter how heavy the bundle on your back may be, or how sweltering the heat, cool pleasures will blow through you here.

And the history of the road keeps marching on before your eyes. Wild Macleods and wild Mackenzies, hurrying to the foray, and waging their little wars, between the sea and the hills. Generations of ghostly men and little children. Raiders from the isles or the hostile shires, stealing silently down the old road, when the moon has dipped behind Boshven, and there is a stillness like death in the glen. But, when they hurry up the road again, driving cattle before them, and carrying their wounded, there is red ruin in the clachan and the sound of keening, where the scattered homesteads stand smoking in the morning sun.

But it is time to go again. So we descend reluctantly into the more civilised region of Flowerdale—a beautiful place with an unpardonable English name. Here are plantations and pine trees, a river, and a glimpse of the chimneys of the Tigh Dige smoking among the trees. On the way down you pass a ruined cottage on the farther side of the glen. Four grey walls and two gaping gables stand on the braeface, with the woods and rocks of Sithean Mhor and Groban making a splendid background. It is the picture of what has been and what will never be again in these remote Highlands—a heart-breaking coronach in stone.

Then the woodman's yards, and evidence of those new Highland clearances which began with the Great War. Across the stream is the ancient Island of Justice, now a green mound, close by the place on which stood the original Tigh Dige, or stank house, of the Mackenzies. And here at last is what was once the Old Inn, by the side of the bridge where the river falls into the sea. With the yellow wrack the old road comes to an end. But just round the corner, when you top the rise of the new road which leads to the north, the green hollow of Leabaidh na Ba Baine, or Bed of the White Cow, lies at your feet. When you lift your eyes from that hallowed spot you will catch a glimpse of the Hebrid Isles lying like a cloud on the rim of the shining sea.

XIV

PREACHING CAVES

BY THE WESTERN SEA

It is many years since I first stood in the oldest preaching cave in Scotland and took a drawing of the little crosses which are carved on its rocky wall. After a good trudge from Whithorn, I found the cave of St Ninian beneath a samphire-covered cliff on the shores of Luce Bay, not far from Glasserton and Monreith. As Ninian came to this district some time in the fourth century, tradition, if not authentic history, has associated his name with the cave for over fifteen hundred years. That is enough to make any man of imagination thrill with holy thoughts as he stands alone in this remote spot and fingers the little crosses.

When Dean Stanley was preparing his lectures on the history of the Church of Scotland, he stayed at Monreith, and visited this Hermit's Haunt in 1871. On that occasion an incised cross was found on the west side of the entrance. Within the next few years other crosses were found, and after several feet of rubbish had been cleared away a stone pavement was revealed. On one of the paving stones a rudely-cut inscription was discovered, of which this fragment was clearly made out: SANCT NI . . . P.

Since fingering these crosses in St Ninian's cave I have travelled many roads and visited many crosses and caves, from grey Galloway to the far Orkneys, and yet, when standing in any primitive place of preaching, my thoughts always fly back to this Hermit's Haunt on the Bay of Luce.

Not many years after that I came upon another preaching cave farther north, by the shores of green Argyll. This time I knew and talked with the lay preacher who had transformed his cave into a rude chapel—John Campbell of Ledaig, the Bard of Benderloch. But, alas, none will ever enter this preaching cave again, for, when the railway was pushed beyond Loch Etive, the cave was altogether destroyed.

Beneath the huge rock nestled the thatched cottage of John Campbell. Nature and the soft climate of Argyll have greatly favoured this little bit of legendary land, and his garden was prodigal with fruits and flowers. Mimulus, pansies, rosemary, sweet william, convolvulus, and heaps of roses grew side by side. Through his beloved flowers came the Bard to offer welcome. He was a man of medium height, well up in years, with keenly-cut Celtic features, and a mild, beautiful eye. It was a pleasant thing to listen to the lilt of the soft voice, but pleasanter still to think of the man who lived and wrote and preached for forty years in this far-away retreat.

Crossing the road we entered another garden which had been made by his own hand, on the top of a large rocky platform. At the foot of this bluff the sea was breaking. Wending our way through the flowers, we followed him down some steps in the very centre of the garden to a low-placed door. Passing through the door, we found ourselves in a large rock-hewn cave. A small window faced the sea, and gave glorious views of Mull. At one end there was a rudely-built fireplace, with a shelf or two of books, and at the other end stood a table made from an oak tree under which Robert Bruce is said to have rested after the Battle of Bannock-burn. All round the walls were wooden benches sufficient to accommodate fifty people. The floor of the cave was laid with planks of wood.

This cave was the poet's chapel. Here he preached the Word for the best part of a lifetime, and taught the younger people of the district know-ledge of the great things of life. Often as the little company sat to hear or stood to sing, the breakers would pound against the rocks and drench the window with spray. Here came not only the neighbours in winter-time to worship, but here also came many great folks in summer to visit the Bard, as a glance at his visitors' book revealed. John Stuart Blackie was a frequent friend. For John Campbell himself wrote much poetry, both in Gaelic and in English. He lived all his life at Dunvalanree, where Ossian held his Feast of Shells, in music-haunted Selma, by the shores of the sounding sea.

But these things all belong to the past. The Bard is long since dead. The rock on the shore, the garden, and the cave itself have all been blasted away. But the memory of it remains, like a whiff of rosemary, fragrant and haunting.

From the time of St Ninian down to times which are within the memory of one or two who are still living, Scots folk have had to worship God in some strange places. But, the more they were opposed, the more determined were they to seek out some natural sanctuary. The most Mosaic place of worship known to me was not a cave, but the Floating Kirk of Loch Sunart—that long arm of the sea which separates Ardnamurchan from the storied land of Morven.

In 1843, when the people of Sunart could obtain no site from the proprietor for a place of worship, they conceived the novel idea of having a floating tabernacle which could be anchored out in the loch, where no landlord could prohibit. At a cost of £2000 a huge iron hulk was built on the Clyde and fitted out with a pulpit, benches, and a small vestry. The ship had comfortable sitting accommodation for 750 people. This extraordinary kind of Noah's Ark was towed all the way from the Clyde, round the Mull of Kintyre, and up the stormy west coast to Loch Sunart, by one or two tug-boats. Sometimes the floating kirk was crowded. At all times the attendance was registered by a scale of feet marked on the stern of the boat, so that a very little arithmetic was needed to determine whether there were four, five, or seven hundred people at worship on a Sunday. Occasionally, when a storm sprang up during a service, both preachers and listeners were greatly moved.

There never was a ship constructed on the Clyde so like the Ark as the Floating Kirk of Loch Sunart, with its bluff barge-like foundation, its whole deck space filled with a square house, having sloping roof, windows fore and aft, and in both port and starboard sides.

There still exists a picture of its arrival in the loch, with the setting sun behind the tug-boat towing the Ark of the Covenant, while two black-coated men stand on the shore and marvel at the curious spectacle. Here was the same spirit that made men gather in caves and dens of the earth to worship God when no stately temple was available.

Recently I came on two other primitive temples on the shores of Wester Ross.

The first is near the township of Sand of Udrigil, on the beautiful bay of Gruinard. You take the road from Poolewe past Aultbea, and cross the moors by Laid. The views across Gruinard on a fine summer day are nothing short of celestial. Just before dropping down to the shores of Gruinard you pass on the left the ruined Chapel of Sand of Udrigil, an ancient holy place standing in a crowded graveyard, and then a little way along the road you come to a well-marked path, all grass-grown now, but once a causeway leading to the shore.

Follow this old road and it will lead you down some rough stone-built steps to a shingle beach, where the great waves break, sucking the pebbles down with a rattle as each roller recedes. Weird stacks of rock stand out of the water like rugged sentinels. Here you will find a large cave which has been hollowed out by the restless waves in a crack of the sandstone cliff. A little wall is built

AN TEALLACH—A RETROSPECT

in front of it, but the entrance is quite open now, although it was once fitted with a doorway which had a lock and key.

Long ago this cave was used by the worshippers of the Free Church. It is large and roomy, receding far into the cliff, but the inner part is low and difficult of access. What a romantic spot for worship! With the sea breaking upon the pebbly beach in sunshine or storm. Many a time the preacher must have had to raise his voice to overcome the sound of the pounding seas.

Alongside of this preaching cave you will find a smaller one. Here, for a long time, an old woman lived with a girl for her companion. Her fire was on the left by the entrance, the bed was on the right, and the front was built up with stones and turf. The only literature which the old woman possessed was a Gaelic Bible.

But the most complete specimen of a preaching cave known to me is far up the west side of Loch Ewe. The road from Poolewe wanders for eight miles northwards along the shore. Here is an absolutely unspoiled bit of crofting country, and the very names of the townships through which you pass have a sough of those Norse and Celtic races which mingled their blood here in far-off times. Boor, Naust, Inverasdale, Smo, Mellan Gauna, Cove—all well-kept, bien-looking crofts, with good houses, and here and there a bunch of Highland shelties on the heather. The road is narrow, and there are six or eight gates to open and shut between Poolewe and Cove. But to me that only adds merit to this road, for here you are perfectly safe from the racing motorist or the eyeless tripper who speeds from hotel to hotel in search of food.

At Smo there is a beautiful bay with a sweep of yellow sand. About a mile farther on you come to another bay called Camus allt Eoin Thomais. Beyond this lies the township of Cove, which is a scatter of cosy crofts behind a bluff headland called Sron-nan-oban, or the Nose of the Little Bay.

Cross the hayfield between the road and the sea, follow the path through a flowery meadow till you come to some steep natural stone steps, and you will find yourself on a shore of shingle and rugged rocks. Turn to the left, and the dark opening in the rocks, screened by greenery and ferns, is the entrance to the cave.

It is a wide, roomy, high-roofed cave, and you descend into it by one or two stone steps. But the unique feature of this cave is, that a wooden pulpit still stands on the north side, faced by a row of rough wooden benches, with bookboards attached. There must have been more seats at one time, and I am told there was a wooden floor. The entrance is roughly built up with stones in the usual way, and little festoons of ferns hang from the roof.

What a picture the imagination paints as you stand and look round! You see the preacher in the pulpit, and the people on the benches, within this strange rock temple not made with hands. You hear the wail of the Gaelic Psalms, the lilted line, and the chorus of men's and women's voices singing in solemn unison. Outside, the waves are breaking with a holy husheen on the sunlit shores, and the far view of the blue mountains makes a finer parable of heaven than any words of a preacher ever can. How long the pulpit and the benches have stood there, or when the last sermon was preached in this hallowed spot I cannot say. But in the silence of this cave there is still a sound of Gaelic singing to those who have an ear which leans fondly to the drones of time.

But I have memories of more than that at Cove on the shores of Ewe.

I can still see the spotless interior of the cottage where the kettle was boiled; the pure white walls and rafters; the snowy fireplace where the peats were blazing; and the kettle hung on the sworlie. I can see also the unrivalled range of hills in Ross and Sutherland—that unbroken panorama of peaks, dim and elusive, from the point of Stoer and Suilven to the giants of Torridon—Eighe, Liagach, and Alligan. I can see the bright green machair lands of Ewe, the yellow sands and the sparkling seas at my feet, as I stand on the height of Sron-nan-oban and watch the waves grumbling below me on the black rocks, or surging through the natural archway of a great stack. I can see the old derelict house on the roadside with its curious crow-stepped gable, abandoned as if some sudden plague had stricken the tenants. The quaint wooden canopy over the fire; the swee still in its place; dishes left on the dresser; a table, a stool, and a settle overturned; the wooden shot-bolt in the door; the straw-strewn floors; and the very picture-cords hanging from the walls!

It was our last day in Ross. But, amid all the sunshine and beauty, the laughter and pleasant company, I could hear the end of an old song, and the last long drawn-out notes of a pibroch. A sea wind blew about us as we turned to look back, and the very breeze seemed to be laden with lost notes:

> O wind, O mighty, melancholy wind,
>   Blow through me, blow!
> Thou blowest forgotten things into my mind,
>   From long ago.

Tods Hunter.

XV

THE FINDING OF RED RIVER

AN ADVENTURE IN FRIENDSHIP

I LOST him on a lochside years ago, somewhere in the region of Tummel and Rannoch. He was an orra man *de luxe*, the complete ghillie, an all-round sportsman, with a few other talents that need not be mentioned. We took to each other at the first glance, before we were prejudiced by names or any such trivial personalities. Indeed, if there were no social ranks in this conventional world, but only human affinities, some of us would be oxtering queer characters.

His real name was Willie. But we called him Red River, because he had spent some years on a ranch in the Red River Settlements. His stories of Red Indians would make a boy's hair stand on end. He had also been in the Army, in the Navy, in the American Rockies, and on the veldt in South Africa. I find in an old notebook something about taking a deer noiselessly with a hook and a bunch of corn. But the details of this extraordinary proceeding would not be profitable either to the public or to the proprietor of a deer forest. The note, however, was evidently written after my first meeting with Red River, although it is not always safe, even for a Scot, to draw an inference.

I

After my departure on that occasion my host asked Red River what he thought I was. He made a guess at several brilliant occupations, but in every case was wide of the mark. When at last the real truth was told him, his conscience smote him painfully as he ran over some of our private conversations; but, regaining himself, he said with a reckless twinkle in his eye:

"Well, it disna matter; he was a cheerie devil, anyway!"

From that day to this I have loved Red River, and have looked for him up and down Scotland. But he was too independent a gangrel to stay long in any one spot of earth. So, at last, I had to write him down on the tablet of my memory as— "Gone—leaving no address."

Last summer I was wandering all alone on a Ross-shire road which skirts the shore and has a fine view of Skye. Between the road and the sea a little wooden shack stands on the turf. Many a time I looked in at the window, and the oftener I looked the more I was interested. It was so small, so tidy, and so evidently occupied by a man who had a place for everything, but who lived the frugal life of a solitary. On this particular day I met a young collie that I did not know, and was bending over the dog in a long conversation. A shadow fell on the road, and when I looked up I saw that an elderly man had come out of the shack. He stood there staring at me with a most beatific smile on his face.

"Do you no' mind of me, sir?"

"Red River! Red River!" I cried.

Men certainly were not given faces for nothing.

"I knew you were here, sir.   For I heard the pipes.   But have you brought yon wee catapult?"

I answered Red River with one eye, pulled something out of my doublet, and in a moment we were inside the shack like brother conspirators.   Then the *ceilidh* began, and it was as if the years between Rannoch and Ross had never been.

He had come back, like many another Highlander, after a lifetime's wanderings, to end his days on the old family croft.   He built this shack on the shore, and so kept his independence; but he was also within cry of the old roof-tree where his mother had taught him to toddle; so he was at home. There are Celts, like himself, who have wandered to the ends of the earth.   Some of them come back again, and some never return.   But not one of them can think of the old home without a yearning to be there.   So, with an old boat, Red River pursues his ancient trade of fisherman in the waters where he first caught flukies with a rusty hook and a home-made line.   He had broken his arm some weeks previous to this, but he is a clean healer, and it did not seem to incommode him unless when he was heaving the anchor.   He bathes in the sea all through the summer and winter.   When the shores are gripped with frost, the crofters, who are not lovers of cold water, say to each other ·

"Look you—Willie must be wanting to die."

But Red River has no thought of dying.   He is full of the joy of living.   He has only learned the secrets of good health—fresh air, plenty of exercise, cold water, and frugal feeding.   So, to-day, he is a

whippy old man, with apple cheeks and a clear eye.
But, after all his wanderings, he has come home.

What stories must be told in that little shack by
the sea on the dark winter nights when the tiny
bench by the fire is crowded, and the place is full
of tobacco reek, and the tale goes round, and
another peat is thrown on the fire! Old escapades
when they were all boys in the little school along
the lochside. Great stories of the fishing at sea, of
deer on the hill, of the long desolate moorlands to
the north where the black bothies are still so hard
to find, and of dark nights spent silently at the
river mouth over yonder, where only yesterday I
saw a silver salmon splashing in the sun.

But the story I like best is his tale of the Red
Indian horse thief.

Sixteen horses were missing from the ranch.
Red River and two other cowboys were sent to
track the thief and round up the horses. Each
took a different route over the hills, with one day's
rations. They were away for three days without
getting on the track of the thief. At last Red
River reined in his horse on a rocky summit and
scanned the lower ground. He noticed a white
spot a good way off. Just then two bullets
whizzed past his ear. Raising his rifle he fired at
the white spot, but it moved off. Then he fired
at a dark spot alongside. There was no reply after
that. So he rode down and found the sixteen
horses hidden behind some rocks. The dark spot
was the wounded Indian, who lay scowling at him,
while his white horse grazed peacefully by his side.
Red River attended to the wounded man, rounded

CANISP, SUILVEN AND CUL MHOR

up the horses, and took the long trail home. The other two cowboys found the Indian later on, and robbed him of three hundred dollars. When they reached the ranch they waved the money in Red River's face with a laugh. He felt a bit sore, but bided his time.

Very soon after that they were sent out to find eleven horses that had been stolen. But, before leaving the ranch, Red River dealt with the two cowboys separately. Covering each in turn with his revolver, he gabbled Gaelic curses over them and made each hand him fifty dollars. So he got his own back, and on this second trek there was no plunder.

One day I trysted Red River to go afishing with us. His way with fish was wonderful, and he knew every bank in the loch. After pulling fish into the old boat almost to weariness, we began to talk of the birds. It was a perfectly calm afternoon. One bird was sailing on the water a considerable way off.

"Could you hit that one, sir?"

It was a long shot, and I pulled out the catapult with fear and trembling, lest I should fail before the old man. But in all cases of high emergency the only thing to do is to appear utterly indifferent. So I selected my best stone, raised the sling, did not hang on the aim, and let fly. We all heard the thud of the stone against the bird. Red River was wild with excitement, but no one got a greater surprise than myself. I had the sense, however, not to try again, and put away the deadly weapon with supreme indifference.

When we got to the shore, his nephew was waiting to help us with the fish. Red River poured out a perfect epic on the catapult, and ended his fiery description with this generous hyperbole :

" Yes, and he never misses. He never misses ! "

Having won this utterly false reputation, I slunk home with the fish, a very humble man.

O Red River ! I am far from the shack on the shores of Ross. But you are like many another wayfaring man whom I have met on that road which none can ever err in loving. You have heard the call that many an exiled heart is hearing to-night, in the far lands beyond the tropic seas— the call of mountain and glen, islands and seas, hearth and home. You will be happy now to the end, because the waves that hushed you to sleep in your cradle will hush you to sleep when the last night falls. You have come back. But they will never return. Somewhere in far Rhodesia there is a Scot who has found a plant on the veldt whose root when burning smells like peat. He goes out to gather it, and throws it on the fire when his brother Scots arrive. But for you the peats lie round your door, and the blue reek rises daily like the fragrant incense of home.

There's a wee, wee glen in the Hielan's,
    Where I fain, fain would be ;
There's an auld kirk there on the hill-side
    I wearie sair to see.
In a low lythe nook in the graveyard
    Drearily stands alane,
Marking the last lair of a' I lo'ed,
    A wee moss-covered stane.

There's an auld hoose sits in a hollow
  Half-happit by a tree ;
At the door the untended lilac
  Still blossoms for the bee ;
But the auld roof is sairly seggit,
  There's nane now left to care ;
And the thatch ance sae neatly stobbit
  Has lang been scant and bare.

Aft as I lie 'neath a foreign sky
  In dreams I see them a'—
The auld dear kirk, the dear auld hame,
  The glen sae far awa'.
Dreams flee at dawn, and the tropic sun
  Nae ray o' hope can gie ;
I wander on o'er the desert lone,
  There's nae mair hame for me.

CHARLES MURRAY.

SUTHERLAND

XVI

WANDERINGS IN SUTHERLAND

A CURE FOR WINTER WEARINESS

WITH the first dawn of April I made for the North.
The winter was past. A burst of bird music floated
in at the open window and wakened me. Like
an arrow from a bow I sped from crowds to solitude, and ere nightfall I was wandering among the
islands of the Ness. The next day I gazed once
more on the glorious view up Strath Oykell from
Invershin Station, and within an hour was on the
road that leads for fifty miles through the wilds of
Sutherland to the blue waters of the West. That
night I fell asleep to the sound of waves breaking
on the shore. But the wanderlust was on me,
and I knew that there would be no peace of mind
until I stood looking out on the seas of Wrath
with the winds from the Arctic blowing about
me.

To every man his own thoughts of any land.
As I travelled over the hill road from Lairg to
Rosehall, on the Oykell River, Sutherland meant
to me, that April day, a sanctuary of solitude, a
geological hammer, and the Marquis of Montrose.

Montrose! It was over this very road that the

great Marquis travelled south one April day in 1650, with a gather-up army of 1200 men to make his last stand at Carbisdale. Publicly disowned, but privately encouraged by his double-dealing master, Charles II., Montrose saw his little army surprised and cut to pieces by Strachan's cavalry. After the rout, and with several wounds on him, he wandered westward, disguised as a countryman, through the trackless desert for two days and nights without food. On the third day he ventured to beg some bread and milk at a herd's shieling. The hue and cry was soon out, and he was captured by one of the servants of Neil Macleod of Assynt. Assynt himself knew that the head of Montrose was worth enough gold to set up his impoverished family for good. So on 30th April he confined the Marquis in his dungeon at Ardvreck Castle, on the shores of Loch Assynt. The ruin on the road close by the Loch is Calda House, a mansion built by the Mackenzies in the seventeenth century; but yon stark wall on the spit of land is all that is left of Ardvreck. Scots memories are long, for here am I calling down a malediction on Neil Macleod of Assynt, and lifting my bonnet to the gallant Marquis. Be a man's sympathies with Covenanter or Cavalier, none will deny that Montrose was one of the greatest soldiers of history, and that it is a dastardly thing for any man to betray friend or enemy for the sake of money.

All the way up Strath Oykell to Loch Assynt I was thinking of Montrose and Neil Macleod, and of two poems. The one was by Ian Lom, the Highland bard:

> Neil's son of woeful Assynt,
>   If I in net could take thee,
> My sentence would condemn thee
>   Nor would I spare the gibbet.
>
> Stript tree of the false apples,
>   Without esteem or fame or grace ;
> Ever murdering each other,
>   Mid dregs of wounds and knives.

The other poem was by Montrose himself, and it is one of the purest lyrics ever written :

> My dear and only love, I pray,
>   That little world of thee
> Be governed by no other sway
>   Than purest monarchy.
>
> He either fears his fate too much
>   Or his deserts are small,
> That dares not put it to the touch
>   To win or lose it all.
>
> But if thou wilt prove faithful, then,
>   And constant to thy word,
> I'll make thee glorious by my pen
>   And famous by my sword.

O Neil Macleod ! What thought you and your lady wife of Lemlair when the body of that gallant cavalier was dismembered in Edinburgh, the limbs sent to the chief towns in Scotland, the head spiked on the Tolbooth, and the body buried beside the gallows on the Boroughmuir ?

> Death wrapping to thee, base one ;
>   Ill did thou sell the righteous,
> For the meal of Leith,
>   And two-thirds of it sour.

The wild west of Sutherland has given rise to many geological controversies. The floor of the whole region is laid on the oldest rocks in Great Britain—the Lewisian Gneiss. My first view of Sutherland, long ago, was from the sea. Seen from a ship's deck, the whole land seems to rise out of the water in bare rounded domes of rugged rock, which tumble over each other like mountainous waves, as far as the eye can reach. Above this wilderness great mountain masses stand sentinel. Without a tree or bush to break the grassless monotony, these rounded bosses have been worn smooth by the ice, and huge blocks of rock—the débris of the glaciers—are poised on the very top of the dome-like hills. Such is the floor of Sutherland. But what of the mountains ?

I climbed to a high top north of Scourie on a clear April day and saw the whole panorama of Sutherland and Ross. The giant mountains stood up from the rolling floor—Ben More Assynt, Glasven, Quinag, Canisp, Suilven, Cul Mhor, Cul Beg, with the outline of the Coigeach hills on the south. The long low point of Stoer stretched westwards into the Minch, and the Old Man of Stoer stood at the very nose of the promontory like a mighty sentry keeping watch. Some of these mountains, like Quinag, show three distinct groupings of rock—the primeval gneiss below ; the horizontal bands of warm-coloured Torridon sandstone above ; with white quartzite wreathing the summit. Seen from the sea, Suilven stands up like a precipitous sugar loaf. Ben Stack is a pointed pyramid of gneiss. Ben Clibrick is one imposing mass of schist. Ben Loyal, with its four pointed tops further north, is a picturesque mountain of granite.

But the geological miracle of Sutherland is the extraordinary series of upthrusts of archaic gneiss, which have not only been forced from beneath thousands of feet of overlying strata, but have been pushed bodily over these strata, sometimes for a distance of at least ten miles. These rocks have been heaved up, thrust over, and crushed together by the action of colossal natural forces.

Had a traveller only time enough, he could pick up a story in every place-name in the Highlands. For example, when I was warming myself at the fire in the little fishing inn at Altnacealgach, on Loch Borralan, I remembered that the very name, *Alt-na-cealgach*, meant the Burn of the Cheat. Here the county of Ross makes a strange wedge-like invasion northwards into Sutherland, as far as Conaveall and the slopes of Ben More Assynt. The truth is, that a dispute took place here long ago as to the boundaries of the two counties ; and when certain witnesses were called they maintained that while they were walking the boundaries they had never wandered a step off Ross-shire ground. Neither they had. But they had first filled their shoes with Balnagowan earth ! Hence, Alt-na-cealgach, the Burn of the Cheat.

The roads in the west are narrow and rough. Perhaps the worst road in Sutherland is that which runs over from Skiag Bridge, on the shores of Loch Assynt, to Kylesku. When I crossed it the day was heavenly. The serrated ridges of Quinag stood blazing against the sky, like a wall of the world.

QUINAG FROM KYLESKU

On the Kylesku side there is a hairpin bend a few miles above Unapool. At this bend two men were repairing the track. They had dug a long trench on one side of the road, and were filling it in with a series of heaps made up of great stones. As we approached they began to flatten out the heaps, that we might pass more comfortably over what would then be something like a river bed. The remaining part of the road was too narrow for any car. But while I was wondering how long it would take, the man at the wheel took my breath away by driving right over these miniature moraine heaps in the trench. Not a word was spoken, and we came through without a mishap. But I thought of the billiard-table roads of the south.

Another road in Sutherland provided a splendid thrill. On the east side of Loch Erriboll there is a nasty steep hill, with neither parapet nor fence on the seaward side, which falls away abruptly to the shore. At the top of this hill there is a rocky bluff round which the road turns suddenly, so that it is impossible at this dangerous corner to see what is beyond. We were creeping up the road and round this rock at the top, when, like a bolt from the blue and without a sound, a motor-bicycle whisked round the rock, on the wrong side of the road, scooted across the nose of the car, and by a miracle did not skid on the grass and so somersault down the slope to the sea. But somebody ought to have been killed.

All which things I deliberately record to indicate that Sutherland roads are very narrow, very rough, often dangerous, and that only fools rush on where angels hold their breath.

It was at Loch Culag that I sat with my back to the south side of a bracken bank and baked in the sun. On the north side of the bank a clean cold wind was blowing. Above was a blue-white sky. In a little grey wood one warbler was dribbling out music for all the world. The loch below me rippled with laughter in the dazzling light. Beyond the tawny hills the weird sugar loaf of Suilven rose into the April sky with a sprinkle of snow picking out the paralleled rings round the summit.

To the north of Scourie lies the bird-haunted sanctuary of Handa Island. After a walk along the hill-tops I climbed down a little cliff opposite the island, and sat perched above the restless waves, betwixt the sky and sea. The great cliffs were in shadow ; a blue sea stretched away to the uttermost isles ; the churn of the tides broke in white spray at the foot of the cliffs and on the skerries ; Skye, Harris, and the Lews slept on the horizon, and the white-winged birds wheeled and cried about me. Here at last was solitude supreme, and it added to the peace to know that no one on the earth knew exactly where I was.

When I reached Durness I found a village asleep. The store was closed because the store-keeper was at the seed-sowing. The gaunt remains of an hotel stand at the cross-roads, gutted by fire. Nobody was within sight. But it seemed all the better because of the sense of peace that reigned.

At Rispond I hummed the melancholy " Rispond Family Elegy," and recalled Rob Donn's poem about the two miserly bachelor brothers who lived at Rispond, with their hoard of gold buried in the earth within sight of their windows. The breakers were making melancholy music on the sands between the rocks, but no dirge is half so sad as the miser's mistake, which turns this glorious world into a prison cell.

> No wrong had they to any done,
>   Judging by human ken ;
> But, neither had they helped in aught
>   Their needy fellow-men.

Then comes the long round of Loch Erriboll and the Kyle of Tongue. Tongue is a very pleasant place after having been in the wilds of Western Sutherland—a long, narrow kyle of shallow water, with endless stretches of sand when the tide recedes ; a bien-looking village with cultivated fields and woods along the shore ; and the ruin of Castle Varrich crowning the little hill opposite. Only at Tongue did I realise that for ten days I had seldom seen any trees or wandered in any considerable woods. True, at Scourie you will find two palm trees growing in an old garden. But here the birds were singing in the deep-gladed woods, and the road was lined with thick-growing pine trees.

The wanderlust was now satisfied. I had shaken off all the winter weariness. The South was calling once more. So there was nothing for it but to take the long forty-mile trek to Lairg again, by Loch Loyal and Loch Naver. At Altnaharra Inn I loitered among memories of the happy long ago. In a little wood near Loch Shin I heard the whistle of a whaup. But what it meant to me none could ever guess.

What thochts o' the lang grey moorlan'
  Start up when I hear that cry !
The times we lay on the heather brae
  At the well, lang syne gane by.

Yet—even yet—if I wander
  Alane by the moorlan' hill,
That queer wild cry frae the gurly sky
  Can tirl my heart-strings still.

R. WANLOCK REID.

XVII

THE WORSHIP STONES OF EDDRACHILLIS

A WILD TEMPLE

THERE is a lonely place on the shores of Sutherland which will always be a hallowed spot to me. It is one of those little inlets of the sea, or viks, which you will find all round the great Bay of Eddrachillis, and up the desolate coast by Laxford to Cape Wrath. Like the blessed life itself, holiday happiness demands wide views, plenty of sunlight, and a beauty of clouds which only adds to the wonder of this world as God has made it. Here, in Sutherland, all these boons are mine.

Sitting on the top of a grassy headland whose rock-face falls sheer to the sea for 200 feet, the short-sighted eyes of a city man might well be strained in trying to catch a glimpse of infinity. The sea is one vast plane of blue, from the Point of Stoer to the Butt of Lewis, round which the ships sail on and on until they come to the Arctic ice. Farther south the hills of Harris float on the rim of the ocean like the elusive lands of Tir-nan-og. Above these Hebrid Isles a long thin line of pearly cloud stretches from end to end of the summer world. A few miles up the Sutherland

K

coast the nose of Handa is thrust into the sea, and yonder to the south the Old Man of Stoer, the eternal sentry of the island-studded Bay of Eddrachillis, stands at the very point of the long flat headland. Over this long black line of Stoer rise the giants of Assynt.

Far below me the sea is glittering in the sun with ripples of silvery laughter. The only sounds are the call of the seabirds, the bleating of sheep, the croak of a raven among the rocks, the grumble of the restless seas as they break everlastingly at the foot of the cliffs, and the whisper of the summer breeze. The beauty of such a day is a benediction, and peace is borne on the winds of God which blow straight from heaven.

O these northern days! White wings flashing above the deep blue sea, green turf by the yellow sands, grey lichened rocks, and ruddy headlands washed by the restless tides, with peat reek drenching the soft airs that play about the crofts. Would that I could waft the wonder of it all across the world to every exiled Celt who swelters in a tropic clime or dreams of home on the barren veldt.

But there is something of great historic interest lying below the precipice at the head of the little vik. Standing on the high ground looking down into the vik you get another vista out to sea. The flat lands of Stoer, about Oldany and Clashnessie, cut across the picture from cliff to cliff, and in the glittering sea the isles of Eddrachillis are framed between the mighty rocks. Descending the steep path, the first thing that meets the eye is a great tumble of rocks which have fallen from the cliff and blocked the head of the vik. These form a mighty bulwark to the sea, and behind this heap of primeval débris, in a hollow surrounded by grassy braes, lie the Worship Stones. At first sight one might mistake this well-defined circular enclosure of stones for a sheep fank. But no ordinary shepherd would gather his sheep and lambs in such an inaccessible hollow at the head of a vik.

No. This is one of the most interesting of modern ecclesiastical remains in the whole of the Scourie district. It is a veritable Bucht of God. For here, after the Disruption in 1843, when the newly-formed Free Church congregation of Eddrachillis could find no other place of worship, they built this solid wall of stones in the form of an oval shelter, and it became the foundation of their "tent in the wilderness," where they worshipped God, no man making them afraid.

You can still trace the steep winding path—all grass-grown now—which led down into the hollow. Step down it, and where it turns to the right at the bottom you will find an open doorway in the wall facing you. By this door all the worshippers would enter the Sanctuary. Right across the enclosure there is a second doorway in the farther wall, by which the preacher would enter to address the huddled flock of Christ. At the right-hand side of the preacher's door there stands a great flat natural outcrop of rock, which would doubtless serve for a raised pulpit.

What a perfect auditorium! The whole congregation, when in the "tent," would be surrounded by a circle of grassy banks and shattered rocks, with

a canopy of blue sky overhead. In quiet weather
it must have been a very peaceful house of God—
but, in a time of storm, the sound of many waters
and great sea billows behind the fallen rocks must
have well-nigh drowned the voice of the preacher
or the voices of the worshippers as they sang :

> Though hills amid the seas be cast,
>   Though waters roaring make
> And troubled be, yea, though the hills
>   By swelling seas do shake.

The preacher, facing his audience, would see
more than a mass of reverent faces. He would see
the mighty cliff rising on the right and the huge
rocks that had been cast down—literally the rock
of ages which had been cleft from that terrific
bastion of the world. But of the thundering sea
there is not a glimpse, and, standing to-day on the
preacher's rock, one might be far away from the
restless waves, were it not that they are breaking
within a stone's throw on the iron-bound shores.

I have never spoken in a sanctuary where the
acoustics were more perfect. It might be the
theatre of Dionysus at Athens, where you stand on
the lowest level with tier upon tier of seats rising
in circles on three sides. What a place for a
conventicle !

As I measured the circular enclosure—39 feet by
27 feet—I remembered with joy that the old
bitterness of Secession and Disruption in the land
is all over, and that we have now seen a great reunion of Scots Presbyterianism. Shall these Worship Stones, then, mean nothing to us ? Far from

ON THE ROAD FROM KYLESKU TO SCOURIE

it. For, like every Covenanter's grave on a Lowland moor, they only make the history of this land all the more dear to a devout Scot. Wherever we find in these Highland wastes a cup-marked boulder, an old grey cross, a Norse place-name, or a Celtic old word, we know that we are the inheritors of a great past which no wise man can ever forget.

So I sit in the sun within this holy circlet of stones listening to the winds whispering among the rocks, to the seabirds calling over the breakers, and to the old raven croaking far up among the craggy hills, and I hear the voices of the dead raised in a psalm, as they praise God for all His mercies. Then, as I climb down the rocks to the sea-cave close by, where the waves are booming eerily in its innermost recesses, I see an otter creeping stealthily up from the sea to his hidie-hole under a fallen boulder, his sleek body, narrow head, and long tapering tail all dripping with the salt water. So wild, so desolate, yet so sacred, is this little vik to-day—for through the ruined walls of the Worship Stones the winds of memory will blow for ever.

XVIII

HIGHLAND RAIN

ON LAND AND SEA

MANY people have asked me why the sun always seems to be shining when I take my journeys up and down Scotland. For in this land of grey weather, where rain is our common heritage, and the average Scot is accustomed to be wet, there would seem to be something false about descriptions of scenery which is made beautiful by perpetual sunshine and seas that are always blue. Why, then, this constant sunshine ? Because I deliberately pick out the radiant days and believe that but for the rain the Western Highlands of Scotland would not be so famous all the world over for such wonderful colour effects on sea and land. So, like a true lover, I have a fine gift of forgetting when it comes to the dull, grey days.

Highland rain ! To a man who has spent part of every year of his life in some part of the Highlands of Scotland, rain of sheer necessity becomes a commonplace.

To-day, for example, in this little township of North-West Sutherland, we have been prisoners of hope for weeks on end. Despite a few brilliant blinks, rain has become a daily damper to our spirits. After the true Highland manner, the clouds have always been going to clear, and then they have closed in worse than ever. This morning they opened their vial of wrath, and the rain came crashing down on the glass veranda like a judgment. Never within a fairly long memory have I known Highland rain that was so persistent or so terrific. Our thoughts naturally turned to the Flood when, at eleven o'clock in the forenoon, the lamp had to be lit because of the darkness.

There are three orders of rain north of the Highland line. There is the soft, warm, persistent smirr which wraps the hills in mist and wets without injury those who plod on in a pother of clammy heat. There is also the sharp shower—heavy, enveloping, sudden—which makes a man fly for shelter to the nearest rock. But it goes as quickly as it comes, and then, when the sun blazes forth out of the bluest of skies, the hills literally gleam with beauty in the clear shining that comes after the rain. Lastly, there is the constant, never-ceasing, day-and-night downpour which generally lasts for three days, reduces the ardent lover of the open to a state of absolute despair, and fills the Highland kitchen with a whole wardrobe of soaking clothes, dripping stockings, and sodden shoes. For in this land of floods and fountains, the coat has not yet been invented which can be called waterproof.

The soft smirr, the sudden shower, the persistent downpour—these are the three kinds of Highland rain to which those who sail the Western seas and climb the Northern hills have been long accustomed. An artist known to me, whose home is on a Western

isle, makes an invariable practice of boring holes in
the soles of every pair of new shoes he buys, that
the rain may have an easy and immediate exit, and
when he sets off for a tramp or a climb, he usually
walks through the first burn. In all this there is
much wisdom. For the man who is always trying
to avoid puddles can know nothing of the joys of
travel; whereas, there is instant peace of mind for
all who accept the inevitable and realise that there
need be nothing injurious in getting wet.

It is almost unbelievable how suddenly a Highland stream can come down when there has been
a cloudburst on the hills. A man may be walking
quietly by a burn-side, casting a line, and almost
before he is aware a cloudburst far up the mountain-
side may send down a wall of water which will
sweep him off his feet. One such cloudburst took
place at the Burn of the Cheat, close by the Inn of
Altnacealgach, many years ago. The day had been
intensely hot. At four o'clock in the afternoon a
fisher sat on a stone in the dried-up bed of the
stream to cool his hands and feet. The air was
electric, and a peal of thunder came from the
copper-coloured clouds on the hill-top. Then
black darkness set in; the storm burst; and rain
fell in torrents. The burn, which had been almost
dry half an hour before, was now a foaming flood.
The stone conduit could not hold it, so it spread
far and wide over the road and several acres of
fields. Stones were hurled down the hill-side with
terrific poundings. A calf standing in the byre was
half drowned. The fisherman dropped his kilt, a
woman servant and a girl of fifteen took off their

shoes and stockings, and all three plunged through the flood to rescue the young bull which was standing in three feet of water. One pushed him with a pole, while another lassoed him with a rope, and so rescued the terrified beast. Sandy, the landlord's brother, had just waded on to the bridge when the whole arch broke down and he was sent swirling down among the débris to the lochside, where he only saved himself by clinging to the bank. The flood subsided as quickly as it came, and yet not a drop of rain had fallen three miles away.

Sandy's legs were sorely crushed by his accident. So next morning a shepherd who was well known for his surgical abilities called at the inn for a dram. He was asked to operate on the sufferer, and immediately the theatre was prepared. Sandy was set down on a kitchen chair, with his cutty pipe in his mouth, and each bared leg stretched across a pail of hot water. The shepherd searched among the bruises for a vein near the ankle and inserted his rude lancet with a vigorous push which brought a Gaelic yell out of poor Sandy. The patient, however, quietly replaced his pipe and tholed the next jag more philosophically, after which both surgeon and subject pledged each other over a gill of whisky.

But rain on sea is even more terrible than rain on land, and I can recollect one or two wild rain-storms on the Western seas.

The first was on Loch Fyne. The squall was heralded by a blue-black line of hissing water that came nearer and nearer with relentless speed. The order was given to take in the big jib and

hoist the storm jib on the little twelve-tonner.
Before the process was completed, however, the
squall was on us. The rain literally lashed the face
so hard that the eyes were blinded and the fumbling
hands failed at first to slip the cleat of the sheets
into the iron eyelet of the jib, which was flapping
in the gale like a thing bewitched. Then followed
a clout on the side of the head with the iron eyelet,
but it was all part of the day's work, and the job
had to be done. At last the jib was secured, the
sheet was hauled taut, and the boat staggered on
through the plunging seas.

Again, it was in the open water between Rhum
and Skye. A strong sea was running, and the
old schooner was thrashing into the storm under
shortened sail. With a long leg and a short
one we were attempting to beat round the Point
of Sleat. The rain never ceased. Great seas
churned past us. For eight hours we were beating
against wind and wave. One cap after another
went overboard. The lee deck was all awash, and
the streaming whips of heaven lashed us without
mercy until we were like drowned rats. When
evening came, we were forced to give in, so we put
about and ran back with a following wind to the
anchorage in Loch Scresort, from which we had set
out in the morning.

And yet there are always compensations. That
is the blessed adventure of bad weather—you never
know what a shower is going to bring you, and I
have made some fine friendships while sheltering
from the rain.

On a certain road in Skye I was caught in one of

those tremendous showers which are brewed among the Coolins, and then pour their largess over the lower lands. There was neither rock nor cottage near-by, so when the deluge came I made for a tinkers' camp which I knew was snugly pitched beside a brawling stream. The day before, I had made the acquaintance of the tinkers and guessed that they were Ullapool men, because they advertised their domicile by the large letters U.L. which were painted on the old brown sail that made their bee-hive tent. In every tinkers' camp in the Highlands you will find an old set of bagpipes, and the sure way to the heart of a piping mugger is to give him a set of old pipe reeds. A little collection of these I carry with me, as a kind of visiting-card in the remote Highlands, for my nomad friends. Having presented a set to one of the Ullapool lads the day before, when he was piping in the village, I knew I was sure of a welcome in the long brown tent when the clouds burst. So I dived into the tent, streaming with rain, and was soon steaming before a roaring stove that made an atmosphere which would have suffocated any but the most robust. How long I sat I know not—for the *ceilidh* was good—but, among a heap of clothes and provisions on which the old bagpipes lay, I noticed one thing with envy.

It was a large loaf of Bilsland's Glasgow bread, all done up by machinery in parchment paper, and sealed with the firm's stamp. Here was something which even a tinker in Skye could get—loaf bread which has left the factory in a clean, waterproof wrapper, and has never once been handled in

transport by dirty hands. Yet in the capital city
of Scotland, so far as I know, no baker can supply
bread which has never been touched by unwashed
hands. When the rain stopped and I stepped out
into the sunshine, I sighed with envy and thought
with a shudder of the bakers' boys in Edinburgh.
What can be done in one city can surely be done in
another.

It is a far cry from Highland rain to a loaf of
bread. This is the twenty-second day on which
we have had heavy rain in Scourie. Here, then,
is the conclusion of the whole matter which an
illustrious Highlander has for ever immortalised in
verse :

> But, if you're a delicate man
>   And of wetting your skin are shy,
> I'd have you know before you go,
>   You'd better not think of Skye.

KYLE OF DURNESS

XIX

HAUNTS OF THE VIKINGS

ROUND THE SHORES OF SUTHERLAND

SITTING alone on this wild headland in the far North, munching bread and cheese, with my bundle lying on the turf beside me, I am watching the restless sea grumbling at the foot of the cliffs which stand like eternal walls on either side of the creek. At any moment a high-prowed ship full of fair-haired Vikings might appear, for in this lone land there is nothing visible at the moment to tell whether you are in the ninth century or the twentieth—no house, no road, no living creature; only the limitless ocean, a few desolate and uninhabited islands, and the white birds flashing above the waves.

I wonder how many Scotsmen realise that for 400 years—from 800 to 1263—the whole of North-West Scotland was ruled by the Norsemen—those consummate sea-rovers who knew every creek or vik on the islands and mainland. They were called Vikings, or Creekmen, because they haunted these viks or inlets of the sea. They conquered the original Pictish inhabitants of the country— although I tremble to discuss who the Picts were —and after four centuries the hardy Norsemen left behind them strange place-names which you will find scattered over the whole of this Sudhr-land, from Oykel to Wrath. For, wherever you come across a Bol, a Vik, a Ness, a Stac, a Cleit, a Geo, a Sgeir, a Tunga, a Dal, a Fjord, a Gil, a Setr an Ob, or a Smoo, there you can be sure that a Viking lived.

Not so many years ago the body of a Viking, a thousand years old, was found encased in ice within the Arctic Circle. Preserved from head to heel, more perfectly than an Egyptian mummy, the body of this Viking, standing upright in a huge iceberg which was cast up on the east coast of Greenland, was discovered by some Danish doctors. Seven feet in height, clad in ancient armour, gripping a spear and shield, the head crowned with the winged helmet of Norse Royalty, the whole figure was dimly visible through the transparent tomb of ice. When the ice was chipped away the Viking looked as if he had died but yesterday ; the hair and moustache long and red and silky ; and the body neither shrunken nor dried up in any way. This wonderful specimen of a Royal Rover was taken to Copenhagen, and the question was immediately asked—Was this the body of Eric the Red, who was famed in saga and rune as a fearless voyager ? For many historians believe that Eric the Red landed on the shores of North America 400 years before Columbus sailed on the little *Santa Maria*. It was this same Viking, Eric the Red, who discovered Greenland (A.D. 985), and as the *Eyrbyggja Saga* tells us, " he called the land which he had found *Greenland*, for he said it would make men's minds long to go there if it had a fine name."

There are five great fjords on the north-east coast of Sutherland, every one of which bears to-day a purely Norse name—Laxford, Inchard, Durness, Erriboll, and Tongue. Of all the five, the wildest are Loch Laxford and Loch Inchard—long deep arms of the sea running into the barren Lewisian gneiss.

How wisely these old Vikings bestowed their place-names! They called the first fjord *Lax-fjord*, that is Salmon-Loch, because they found it full of salmon. And after a thousand years it remains true to its name, for the little Laxford river is perhaps the finest salmon river in the north, and fish are still taken out of it up to a weight of over 40 pounds.

Inchard was the *Engi-fjord*, or Meadow Loch, of the Norsemen. Durness was their *Deer's-Point*. Erriboll was their *Eyrr-bol*, or Beach-Town. Tongue was their *Tunga*, a Tongue of Land.

As I wandered from one clachan to another along the shores of Laxford, right out to the seaboard opposite to the Isle of Handa, I wondered how the half-dozen families in each place found a living. But the sea is full of fish, their little crofts are smiling green in the sun, and doubtless these hardy Northmen of to-day pity us far more than we town folks pity them. Foindlemore, Fanigmore, and Tarbet—these are the happy townlands of many a Celt, both young and old. And for intelligence? Of the two strong lads who rowed me from Tarbet out to Handa, the younger, who was only in his 'teens, used geological terminology in a way that would have put most city lads to shame.

The road to Kinloch Bervie also runs high above Loch Inchard, from one prosperous township to another. From a point where the road rises to a height of nearly 300 feet there are glorious views across the Sutherland wilderness. On the south side of the loch a wild high path leads from Rhiconich to Rhimichie. Indeed, so foreign-sounding are the names of the clachans about Loch Inchard that you might be travelling in another land, and if you ever reach Sheigra, on the Atlantic coast, you may safely say you have come to the end of all things where the only outlook is to infinity.

Returning to Rhiconich, the road leads north to Durness, with wide prospects to Arkle, Foinnaven, and Spionnaidh. Then the wild rocks of Western Sutherland are left behind, and when you have passed Gualin, which means a " shoulder "—the real summit of the glen—you descend to Keoldale Ferry, where you cross the Kyle of Durness for Cape Wrath. You are now in a region of flat sheep lands, green fields, wide waters, and homely hills—the whole reason for this remarkable change of scenery being that you have left the archaic gneiss, and are now in a region of limestone. The ruins of the Pictish towers which line this strath remind you of the ancient inhabitants of the land, who must have greatly resented the invasion of the Vikings.

It was with longing eyes I looked across at Keoldale to the road which leads to Wrath. The Norsemen never bestowed a name with more exactitude when they called that uttermost cliff of Sutherland *Hvarf*—the Turning Point. For in all

BEN LOYAL

their voyages from Scandinavia to the Western Isles these sea-robbers would be glad to turn southwards to the sunny seas when they came to the beetling cliffs of Wrath. Once round Wrath, the Turning Point, and they would be delivered from the treacherous tides and storms of the Pettland or Pictland Firth, which we call Pentland now.

The village of Durness, or the Deer's Point, is an unspoiled clachan. The first time I visited Durness I was a victim of speed. But on this day of sunlit glories I turned westward past the ruined hotel, and came to the place of pilgrimage for all who love the poetry of the Celt, about a mile from the village. It is the churchyard of Balnakeill, where Rob Donn, the celebrated poet of the Reay country, is buried.

I shall treasure to the end of my life my first vision of Balnakeill Bay—an immense sweep of white sand over which the waves were rippling in long green curves, blue waters sparkling in the sun, with an outlook to the Great North Sea between Geo Dubh and Far Out Head. So wide and wonderful, and so far from the madding crowd!

At the head of this beautiful bay stands the old churchyard of Durness with its roofless church, and close by it the bald mansion-house of Balnakeill, which was once the residence of the Bishops of Caithness, who came to hunt on the Deer's Ness, and the residence at a later date of the noble family of Reay. This church was built in 1619 on the site of an older one which was attached to Dornoch Monastery. Doubtless long before that date there was a still older cell of the Celtic Church on this

L

spot.   The ruined walls and the crow-stepped gables are all ivy-covered now, and inside may be seen an old circular font and an ancient tomb with this quaint inscription :

> Donald Macmurchov hier lyis lo.
> Vas il to his freind var to his fo :
> Trve to his maister in veird and vo. 1623.

In this churchyard stands a memorial to Rob Donn, before which all lovers of Celtic literature will uncover the head.   For here was a natural genius who, despite the fact that he could neither read nor write, composed Celtic poems and melodies which were kept alive by tradition, and handed down by word of mouth from one generation to another.

He was born at Altnacaillich, in Strathmore, at the foot of Ben Hope, near the ruined tower of Dornadilla.   What a human combine was Rob Donn !   He was literally cradled in song, for from his mother he inherited the gift of poetry.   As a boy he was most precocious, and had a wonderful power of repartee.   Janet Mackay, whom he afterwards married, had a musical ear and a beautiful voice.   Although Rob Donn was not " out " in the 'Forty-Five, he was a Jacobite poet, and wrote two political songs—one in praise of Prince Charlie, and the other on the shame of the Act which forbade the wearing of the Highland dress.   He was a notorious killer of deer, a fine shot, and an unrepentant poacher.   Indeed, on one occasion, when he was actually going to the Court to be tried for slaying deer, he saw a herd by the roadside, and to

the consternation of his wife could not resist from
shooting two of them.

"Go home," said he to her, "and if I do not
return there will be all the more for you."

His gun was so dear to him that when he was
growing too old for the hill he filled the barrel with
deer tallow, climbed to the top of Ben Spionnaidh,
took farewell of his beloved weapon, and buried it
among the summit rocks of Carn-an-righ, that no
other hand should ever touch it.

O Rob Donn! How well some of us understand you. I often wonder if the gun will ever
be found; for Rob Donn died in 1778, at the age
of sixty-four; and older weapons of the 'Forty-
Five have been found among the rocks. Yet this
poacher poet was such a clean-living man that he
sang the praises of religion, and was appointed
Assessor of Session in his native parish.

His poetry reflects the social life of his time in
songs of the shieling, the harvest, the wool-waulk-
ing, and the drove road. He looked on nature with
a seeing eye. His dirges are full of tears. His love
songs are pure and tender. He abhorred in-
sincerity, and his satires cut like a razor dipped
in oil. For many years after Rob Donn's death
the only library in which his poems were to be
found was the memory of his own people. But in
the year 1829 the first edition of his poems was
printed, and this handsome monument was erected
over his grave by his fellow-countrymen.

All the way to Tongue the Norseman contends
with the Celt in the place-names of this spacious
land. The Smoo Cave, which Sir Walter gazed

at in wonder, lies at the head of a little cove about a mile from Durness; and it was well named *Smjuga* by the sea-rovers, for the name means a narrow cleft to creep through. A mile or two farther on, at a steep turn of the road, you look down on a bay of gleaming sand, and right across the wide waters of Erriboll to far-off Whitten Head —a white towering cliff which is a landmark to sailors. The Vikings called it *Hvitr*, the White Headland; and the Celts called it *Kennagall*, the Headland of the Stranger. Both true. For that cliff will always remain a gleaming cliff; and to the very last day of the Norse occupation, when Haco, defeated at Largs, sailed for the last time round Whitten Head, it was called *Kennagall*, the Headland of the Stranger, by the Celts.

Loch Erriboll is one of the finest harbours in Britain. In this beautiful fjord of clear, deep water a whole fleet could anchor and ride out a gale in perfect safety. When you have circled its shores or taken the shorter way across its calm waters by Heilim Ferry it is but a mile or two over the heather to Loch Hope.

Surely the view from Hope Lodge up the loch to Ben Hope is one of the very finest in Sutherland! And if you follow the road up the east side of Loch Hope for ten miles you will come to Altnacaillich, Rob Donn's birthplace, and to the finest of all the ruined towers in Sutherland, the Dun of Dorna-dilla. Here, long ago, a native king of that name lived. When Haco's ships were anchored in Loch Erriboll, the Norsemen landed to plunder the country-side. But a band of native warriors who

BEN HOPE

were led by an officer of King Dornadilla surprised the raiders, and killed most of the strangers. Among the slain was the Norse commander, whose name was Urradal, and Strath Urradale bears his name to-day. That was the last of the strangers.

All that is a tale a thousand years old. But still we see as in a dream these fair-haired strangers in the blue-eyed, flaxen-headed children of tempest who travel south or cross the storm-tossed Minch from the Outer Isles to seek their fortunes in the cities of the world to-day.

Recently a print appeared in *The Scotsman* of a modern Viking ship — the Raold Amundsen — moored in the Thames opposite the Houses of Parliament. Every one who stepped aboard that perfect reproduction of a Norse galley was stepping across ten centuries of history. For we are still a seafaring folk, and the hardy Vikings whose blood flows in our veins must look with prideful eyes from their Valhalla on the monster ships that are launched from our yards. They knew the wonders of the deep, and their sagas are full of poetry. To them the sea was The Glittering Home. The sky was The Wind Weaver. The wind itself was The Never Silent. The very rocks were The Bones of the Sea. The rain was The Tears of the Clouds, and they called the clouds The Wind Floating. In life the Viking loved his long boat, and after death he was sometimes buried in his ship. Little wonder that his last words were :

> I will go down
> To the steeds of the sea.

XX

THE ISLAND OF HANDA

A BIRD SANCTUARY

My heart went out to Scourie when I came down the hill one April evening and took in at a glance this little unspoiled Sutherland township.

A scatter of white houses ; crofts on the green hill above the sea ; a tiny church, an old lodge among trees, a little bay looking to the sunset, a circlet of white sand with a lonely place of graves above ; the nose of Handa Island making a perpetual rampart on the north-west ; one or two skerries, a restless sea, now sparkling bright as an emerald, now cold and grey, but for ever grumbling round the rocks—that is Scourie.

To watch the sunlight flashing over the Minch between Sutherland and Lewis, or the rain-swept seas lashing white round those desolate islands and skerries which have names on a map but no living inhabitants except the seabirds and the whiskered mild-eyed seals ; no sail on the horizon ; no summer visitors as yet on the mainland to spoil the unbroken life of the crofting townships, or to bring the breath of a fremmit world into these utter desolations—this is to enjoy the blessing of the separate.

There is always something fascinating about an

island, especially if it lies in the lap of the Western seas and floats in the sunset. To live at Scourie is to be always looking out to Handa—from the hills, from the shores, from the fishing banks. It keeps pulling at your heart, until at last you have to take a boat and go out across the sea to explore the mysteries of this lonely island with the wild cliffs.

The first time I visited Handa we sailed out from Scourie on a heavenly day, which had cleared up after a depressing morning of rain. It was in that never-to-be-forgotten August of the thirty days' rain. But the half-dozen days that had sun blinks in them were all the brighter when they did come. The waves rolled in from the Atlantic in long tumbling masses of blue water, and when we got to the outside of the island and were sailing under the beetling cliffs, which rise straight up from the sea like built walls of old red sandstone, the boat was sometimes hidden in the trough of the ocean, and sometimes racing on the crest of a great billow. With a wind blowing fresh from the west, the whole sea was one tumbling mass of restless indigo. On such a day the heart of a sailor sings with joy. All the time we were watching the waves breaking at the foot of the rocky walls. Clouds of white spray searched the red cliffs like showers of snow, while the white birds screamed and whirled with delight along the face of the precipices, like little bits of flashing life in the brilliant blue-white world.

When we came to the Stack of Handa, which is a great mass of isolated rock separated from the main cliff on the north side of the island, the sea

began to moderate, and when we sailed into the
Sound we were in a region of sheltered waters,
with the sun blazing down on the barren shores
of Sutherland and on the white sands of Handa.

The island is low and almost flat on the eastern
side, rising gradually in heathery moors to a height
of 406 feet at the cairn on Sithean Mor above the
cliffs on the western side. The reason for this is
that the whole island is composed of stratified Torridon sandstone, which has been tilted up from the
east and south-east to the west and north-west. It
is about a mile and a half long by a mile across.
One traveller writing on Handa says that " the
Laurentian cliffs of Handa rise in sheer precipices
600 feet above the western sea." But the cliffs
are not quite 400 feet high.

The next time I visited Handa I crossed in a
rowing boat from the little clachan of Tarbet.
This is an ideal excursion, for, if necessary, you
can motor to Clashfern, on the Scourie-Durness
road, or even to Foindlemore, walk to Tarbet, row
out to the island, and after spending some hours
there row all the way back to Scourie.

But whichever way you go to Handa you will
find the sea alive with cormorants, terns, guillemots,
razorbills, puffins, and gulls. In the earlier months
of the summer you will find the ledges of the
cliffs alive with nesting birds. But in August the
breeding-places are almost deserted. The stench
of places like Ailsa Craig, the Bass Rock, and Handa
is anything but pleasant, as those who have visited
those bird sanctuaries know well. But that is only
at the breeding-time.

The great blue-black cormorants stand motionless in little groups on the rocks, very solemn and sentinel-like, as if they were black-coated monks contemplating the mysteries of the deep. Or they fly at enormous speed across the water, with their long black necks stretched out in a straight line. Another name for the cormorants is St Cuthbert's Fowls, for they were the favourite birds of St Cuthbert (d. 687), who lived on Holy Island, off the coast of Northumberland, in the seventh century. That is why the priceless Lindisfarne Gospels have countless cormorants worked into the designs of the illumined pages. These Gospels were inscribed on the Holy Isle of Lindisfarne by Bishop Eadfrith about the year 700, " in honour of God and St Cuthbert," and after 1200 years they remain to-day in an almost immaculate condition within the British Museum. On one page alone there are eighty-eight cormorants worked into the beautiful design. So I never see a cormorant, or skart, winging its way across the stormy sea or standing motionless on a rock but I remember good St Cuthbert, who first saw the vision of Christ in a sheepfold of Lauderdale, and afterwards served God as a missionary to the wild inhabitants of the borders, both at Melrose and on the sea-girt isle of Lindisfarne.

The sands of Handa are white, and the machair above them stretches like an emerald carpet along the shore. At the north end of the machair you will find a sheepfold, a row of ruined foundations, and a tiny graveyard close by. There are only a few upright stones in the graveyard, with one flat table slab on which is carved the name of "Peter Morrison." Farther on there is a solitary shepherd's house without a tenant. That is Handa to-day—a group of ruined shielings, a handful of graves, two hundred shepherdless sheep, a bastion of terrific cliffs all splashed with the lime of sea fowl, gleaming sands on the eastward shores, and the never-ending music of salt sea winds that blow from the lone Atlantic.

And yet there was once a Queen of Handa. In the early years of the nineteenth century there were about a dozen families on the island. They maintained themselves on fish and by taking the eggs of the seabirds. The men were fearless cragsmen, and swung each other over the cliffs on ropes. The oldest widow was always called the Queen of Handa, and she was acknowledged not only on the island but on the mainland as well. Emigration, however, or some other reason, swept the people from Handa, and to-day it is uninhabited.

Charles St John, who wrote his famous "Tour in Sutherland" in the year 1848, describes a somewhat pathetic experience. On approaching Handa he saw a large white cat sitting on the rocks looking wistfully towards the mainland. He also speaks of two shiploads of emigrants on the point of leaving a harbour near Scourie. Handa must have been deserted about that time ; the white cat probably being the stray pet of some of these emigrants, for " all the emigrants had left the island early in the spring for America." So Handa has been a no-man's land ever since the year 1848.

" She is waiting for the ferry," remarked the

boatman as they looked at the white cat.   But—
the ferry never came !

During the nesting season every ledge on the cliffs
is crowded with birds.   Guillemots stand in long
lines wherever there is a footing place, competing
with their second cousins the razorbills.   Countless
puffins hide in the holes at the top of the giddy
heights.   Clouds of birds fly about the face of the
precipices and fill the air with the din of their
calling.   Indeed, so crowded are they in their flight
that one might think a heavy snow shower had
swept across the seas.   It is at once a very beautiful and an awesome sight to stand there and gaze
down at those fearsome cliffs, with clouds of screaming birds about you, and the waves churning themselves into yeasty foam on the deathly rocks far
below.   What a perfect bird sanctuary is this
uninhabited island in the far North, with its un-
scaleable cliffs looking across the infinite seas to the
far-off Arctic ice !

And yet to me scenery is always enhanced by
human recollections.   So I cannot forget the happy
company that gathered on the machair above the
pure white sands ;   the blue-green waters all shot
with sunlight that made a bath of perfect buoyancy
for the long leisurely swim ;   the blazing fire against
the grey rock, where the kettles sang, and our
hunger was more than satisfied ;   the long lazy
rest in the sun when the peace pipe was lit ;   and,
when it was nearly time to go, the shrill skirl of
the bagpipe as a wild reel was danced by young
and old on the fine close-cropt turf.

It is thus that the happy summer days spent by

the sea, among the hills, or in the heathery pine
woods beside a running stream, can never be wholly
lost to us, when the dark days of winter imprison
us in fog-bound streets, or compel some old cam-
paigner to lie abed and suffer the pains of disable-
ment, with many a misty dream of the open road
and the steep ascent.

> Did we brood on our sorrow
>   And see all the future in strife,
> Who would wait for the morrow,
>   Or bear with the bleakness of life ?
>
> 'Tis only the setting
>   Of sorrow that lets us live on :
> The grace of forgetting
>   All else but the joy that is gone ;
>
> In the scenes we remember
>   From months or from years that are by,
> The fogs of December
>   Gleam gold with the sun of July.
>
> GEOFFREY WINTHROP YOUNG.

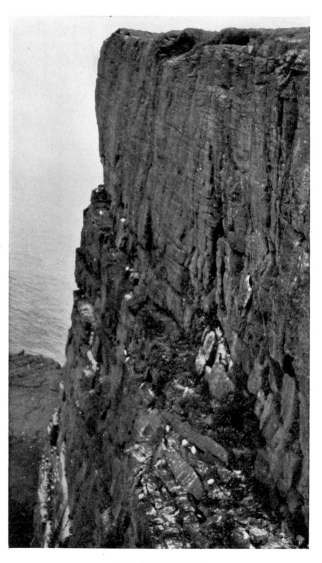

CLIFFS OF HANDA

XXI

THE UNSEEN HOST

AND THE HOUSE OF HOSPITALITY

I DO not understand the man who finds time hanging heavily on his hand, who thinks life dull, or who has a constant quarrel with other people. The road teaches us many lessons, and if we do not learn them the fault is ours. To a wandering man who has eyes in his head, love in his heart, and a dash of humour, time flies, the world is teeming with interest, there is some good in everybody, and the house with the open door is never hard to find.

But there is this in travel for all who take the road—an added element of surprise. You set out every morning on an unknown adventure. The unexpected leaps out on you at every corner. You cease to anticipate to-morrow's programme, for beyond the sunset lies the unknowable. You take the road as it comes—thankfully, expectantly, without worry. You cease to harass yourself even about stopping-places. The world becomes a friendly place. All classes get levelled out. East End and West End mean nothing to those who have to trudge along the dusty path in the heat with all their belongings on their backs. So the tramp can teach the millionaire a great lesson in faith, for while he takes every man as he finds him, he takes no anxious thought for the morrow.

I have had many strange adventures on the road, but until that day in June I never had the mystical experience of being entertained by an Unseen Host in the heart of the Highlands.

I remember a haunting passage in "John Splendid," which describes seven broken men who were flying from the black battle of Inverlochy. One inclement night they stumbled on the empty house of Dalness in Glen Etive, open to the night, with candles lit in the sconces, a wood fire burning in the tapestry-hung hall, an untouched meal laid on the table, and bottles that winked to the flicker of candle and hearth. An uncanny sight for men that were hunted, desperate with hunger, and apprehensive of being dirked at every road end. From the open door and a multitude of little windows light gushed lemon yellow on the lawn. Here was a house of mystery, lit from tolbooth to garret, peat fires banked high, and a fine supper waiting for any gangrel who might step out of the inclement night into comfortable hospitality. So, after some swithering and reconnoitring, the seven men sat down to the feast, and soon their tongues were loosened by generous draughts of wine. Then they boldly threw their glasses on the hearth, shuttered the windows to the lashing storm, and hoped with a certain gaiety that there was no ambuscade. But it was all a trap laid by the Macdonalds for this handful of MacCailein's men. So the ploy ended with dirks and a flight through the storm.

Not so with us.   So far from being broken men, we were four boon brothers housed in a hostelry at Inverness, with the river sparkling in the sun every morning before the open door, and a witching view of the castle turrets bathed in the midnight afterglow.

No man of any historic sense can travel up and down the Great Glen, from Fort-William to Inverness, without many thoughts of battle days.   But the twentieth century is not the seventeenth or the eighteenth, and we have now substituted the broad highway for Wade's old roads, the motorcar for the lumbering coach, the wireless for the local runner, and the telephone for the franked epistle.   Time and space have been annihilated, and all the world knows to-day what is going on in the obscurest corner.

Yet the finest sensibilities are still untouched, and the mysteries have only been deepened.   Far away in England a voice began to speak.   Here, in the North, another answered.   Again and again the voices spoke—one in Cheshire, one in Lochaber, and one in Inverness.   The invisible speaker in Cheshire, whom we had never seen, was to become our unseen host.   Only a *taibhsear* who has the gift of second sight could possibly gauge the degree of mystery that lies in those voices which are passing each other with soundless messages on the hundred thousand winds of the world, like phantom ships in a silent night.

That day we had travelled eleven miles on the old Wade Road, and fished Loch Duntalchaig from morning till night.   When this road was opened in the year 1726 Lord Townsend and one or two other nobles drove over it in a great lumbering coach-and-six, to the astonishment of the natives, who had never seen a carriage on wheels. The Highlanders made deep obeisance to the gorgeous coach-man, but paid no attention to the gentry inside. Indeed, the year before that, an old beldame with a wrinkled face saw the soldiers preparing to move a huge boulder.

"Fools!" she cried, "that stone will be there for ever!"

But when the stone began to move she gave forth an eldritch yell, and ran from the workmen, whom she took for warlocks.

To-day the rumour goes that on the new North Road the ghost of General Wade has been seen wandering about on the still nights, silently examining the gradients and the bridges. But when the wraith stands at the bridges and thinks of his own, he sighs in the summer night for a beauty that is gone. The sighs are heard mostly in the region of Tomatin.

The next day dawned with all the heat and beauty of perfect midsummer. It was over fifty miles to the house of hospitality. But one hundred miles to-day is like an evening stroll to a man with a swift car. I will not linger on the legends by the way. But a man cannot pass by Castle Urquhart without thinking of De Bois and his lady wife keening on the eagle's crag. At Invermoriston the thoughts fly to the eight men who guarded Prince Charlie in the Cave at Corriegoe, and to Mac-kenzie's Cairn. At old Kilcummin many a poor

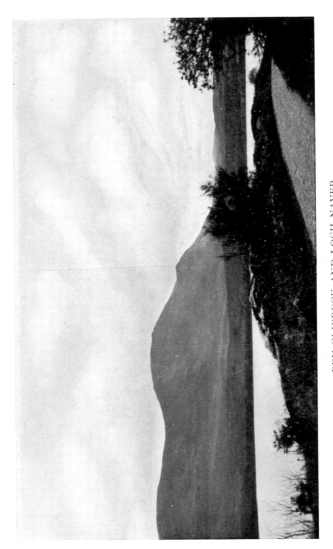

BEN CLIBRECK AND LOCH NAVER

Jacobite languished in the fort. Would that the grey ruin of Glengarry did not remind us of Pickle the Spy ; or Tober-nan-ceann of the seven bloody heads washed in the well. But the moment we enter Lochaber our hearts go out to the gentle Lochiel and Dr Archie Cameron, who lost all for the Prince they would neither betray nor desert. Montrose, Argyle, Prince Charlie, and many a Scots king before them—did ever a high road take us through more history and heart-breaking romance than that which runs from Culloden to Inverlochy ? Every foot of it cries out

> Of old, unhappy, far-off things,
> And battles long ago.

We arrived at noon, turned down a long avenue, and found the door of a great house standing wide open to the blazing sunshine, with all the west windows winking across to Lochiel's sanctuary at Achnacarry. Here, at this earthly paradise, the boon brothers arrived, as did the seven broken men at Dalness long ago, and found the open door, open windows, a feast spread on the table with the choicest of food, the best of drinks, and tobacco to suit all tastes.

But there was no sign of the host ! Yet for us the house was haunted.

Boats rode at the jetty ready for us to step aboard. From room to room we wandered at will. But there was no one in any of them. Empty, luxurious, quiet, soundless, their windows looked on one of the most romantic views in the Highlands. Yonder lay the Dark Mile, that *Mile*

M

Dorcha, which is now no longer dark. Outby, the azaleas made a blaze of colour like a fire, and scented the warm airs most deliciously. But while there was the best of service at the table and Donald at the jetty to do our bidding with the boats and rods, there was no host to be seen anywhere. It was an eerie meal, with many a glance thrown over the shoulder to catch a glimpse of someone who never came.

The long afternoon was spent on the loch fishing for trout that were all asleep. The summer beauty was so hypnotic that it was hard to do anything but dream. The wind fell away, and the wonder of the woods and hills was mirrored in the sea of glass. The romance of the old days and the pathos of the lost cause so gripped our hearts that there was only one way of expressing it. So the gardener's pipes were borrowed, and after a little coaxing the bag was under the oxter, the ear was leaning fondly to the drones, and the whole pageant of history soon was rolling down the loch, waking the echoes of the dead, with "Lochiel's Gathering" for the march of the Cameron men to Glenfinnan, and "Lochaber no More" for the nameless men who died in exile, or among these hills where Butcher Cumberland hunted the remnant like vermin.

It was quite inevitable that two men should land on the shores of Achnacarry and wander for a little while in the old haunts of Charlie and his friends. But there comes a moment when the bravest mood is over, and the heart ceases to feel. So as the white boat carried us back swiftly again to the other shore in the radiant light of the fading day a new port was put on the pipes, and we drew in to the jetty with a perfect riot of Gaelic gaiety. Then the world seemed emptied of all sound when the chanter fell silent and the ribbons fluttered no more.

That evening Nature seemed to be swooning in a dream of peace as we made our way up the shores of the three lochs. When the stars came out the whole day became a parable of that road which is more mystical than any highway the feet of man has ever travelled. Throughout this day of haunting happiness we had been looking for a face that we had never seen, and listening for a voice that we had never heard in the flesh. Yet with what rare delight had our host been entertaining us in his house of hospitality.

Little wonder, then, that to those of us who look on this homely earth as a house of daily delights, and have long ago realised that we are being entertained with a Hospitality that is far beyond our deserts, these words became the epilogue of a perfect day and lulled us to sleep by the side of the running waters :

> Strange the world about me lies,
> Never yet familiar grown—
> Still disturbs me with surprise,
> Haunts me like a face unknown.

WILLIAM WATSON.

XXII

THE TEN COMMANDMENTS OF WALKING

A TRAMPER'S DECALOGUE

THE greatest pleasures are always the simplest, and the finest relaxations of man are to be enjoyed only by those who are content to return to the most primitive methods of travel. Riding a horse, sailing a boat, walking along the surface of this most wonderful world. Be a man as rich as Crœsus or as poor as Lazarus, nothing will ever take the place of these particular forms of oper-air recreation.

But in this age of hurry I fear that walking—the slowest of all the methods of travel—requires some recommendation. Let me, therefore, state the Ten Commandments of Walking, for all who are about to throw the rucksack over their shoulders and set out for a tramping holiday on the summer roads.

The First Commandment is—THOU SHALT WALK, IF THOU WOULDEST KEEP WELL.

Walking is the healthiest exercise in the world. Let a man be ever so strong, there is no hope for his body unless he takes plenty of exercise in the open air. Walking is the best of all physical economies. It clarifies the mind, and exhilarates the spirit, just because it keeps every organ in the body working in a normal state of health. Thought and feeling are largely determined by the physical condition of the man who thinks and feels. For all, therefore, who would come home from a holiday fit for work, happy-hearted, and mentally alert, this is the First Commandment—Thou shalt walk.

The Second Commandment is—THOU SHALT SET OUT PROPERLY EQUIPPED.

Travel light. Let your shoes be stout old friends. Eat little while you are tramping, drink less, and have no fear of the sun, the rain, the wind, or the weather. Carry everything on your back, in a rucksack that is properly slung, and in the hand nothing but a stick to swing rhythmically to your whistling or your songs, or to strike at a pebble or a dog, if you are attracted to the one or attacked by the other. And for clothes—let them also be like true friends, old, comfortable, weather-beaten.

The Third Commandment is—THOU SHALT HAVE NO PROGRAMME.

Let each day determine itself. There is no irritation like that of being compelled to walk to an exact time-table. Set out every morning from your inn with any determination you please—having paid your bill, and eaten heartily—but turn aside anywhere, and at any moment, to see some great sight, or to tickle the lusty trout; sit down when you will; retrace your steps, even, if you wish to see the great sight again; explore the by-ways at all costs; and you will have some hope of happiness. But hurry not for the mere sake of getting there.

In the folly of youth I once walked thirty-six miles in one day, and limped other twenty the next. But be not deceived, no man can see the world properly who is either in a hurry or in pain. Therefore, have no programme, no time-table, and no anxiety about the mileage.

The Fourth Commandment is—WITH ALL THY WALKING THOU SHALT GET KNOWLEDGE.

Knowledge comes through the eyes, the ears, and all the senses. But many a man looks without seeing, hears without really listening, feels without being able to interpret. I have travelled in a swift car through the sublimest scenery for a whole day, looking on the most moving sights without seeing them, passing birds and beasts that I love with all my heart, but never getting a chance either to watch them or to listen to the magic of their music—a prisoner at heart all the time, to whom all natural desires are forbidden. Then I have started out to walk slowly over the same road, taking a week to cover the ground, alone, and I have gained knowledge of men and places, seen at leisure a thousand things I would otherwise have missed, and listened quietly to the music of wood-land, wind, and sea. Therefore, with all your walking see that you get some understanding of the wonders of the world through which you pass.

For as the writer of *Ecclesiasticus* says : " The wisdom of a learned man cometh by opportunity of leisure, and he that hath little business shall become wise."

The Fifth Commandment is — THOU SHALT CHOOSE THY COMPANIONS OF THE ROAD WITH THE UTMOST DISCRETION.

I once spent fourteen days in a small canoe, touching my companion with every movement of the body, knowing that each motion of arms or legs meant something vital, of pleasure or pain, in wind or wave, whether sailing or paddling : but we were well chosen ; so the memory of that fortnight has remained a lifelong joy. But had there not been a perfect rapport between us we would certainly have quarrelled, and found a watery grave through sheer incompatibility or fed-up-ness. So is it with walking. Refuse to walk with everybody or anybody. Choose your companion of the road as a wise man would choose his wife. Rather travel alone than ill-mated. The longest road can be a perfect idyll to a solitary rambler. But every milestone reminds you of the next when your fellow-traveller is a bore.

The Sixth Commandment is—THOU SHALT NOT DESPISE THE PASSER-BY.

The road is the most democratic institution in the world. It belongs to everybody. It belonged to the world and his wife long before the time of Abraham, and even he, like a true tramper, went out not knowing whither he went. The road will belong to the public to the end of time. The greatest honour in humanity is to be a common wayfaring man, and no one meets the human ordinary more frequently than the tramp. Despise no one. Pass the time of day with all. Ask no names and seek no introductions. Share your matches or your bread with your fellow-vagabonds. You will find them full of surprises, as doubtless so will they find you. And the best safeguard against aggression is a little touch of kindness. One half of the world does not know how the other half lives. That is the tragedy. But this is the glory of the road—that it belongs to all, it introduces us to all sorts and conditions of men, and levels all ranks by the sheer necessity of circumstances. It bestows its blessings of wind and weather, beauty and companionship, on the good and the evil alike. Therefore, despise no one.

The Seventh Commandment is—THOU SHALT NOT DESTROY ANYTHING THAT IS THY NEIGHBOUR'S.

Wild flowers by the hedgerows ; song birds in the woods ; fish in the most tempting pools ; heather on the hills ; standing grain with the wind-waves rustling through it in the autumn sunshine ; these are God's gifts to the wayfaring man. Enjoy them all, but destroy none. Neither shall you light fires against tree trunks, or leave them smouldering when you depart. A careless match has often set a hill-side ablaze, and an empty bottle left among the bent grass or the heather will focus the sun like a burning-glass, and so fire a whole plantation. Every time you do some damage on the road you dishonour your comrades. Therefore, leave no litter. Cover up your tracks. But, above all, destroy not anything that is your neighbour's.

The Eighth Commandment is — THOU SHALT OFTEN KEEP SILENCE IF THOU WOULDEST HEAR WHAT THE VOICE OF NATURE HAS TO SAY.

Until you can pass through the world quietly, you will never learn anything. The democracy of this new age has obtained a wondrous freedom. But when man in his first state of ignorance is let loose in the natural world he straightway celebrates his freedom with a yell. I remember walking in Switzerland long ago with a little Scots philosopher who has since then been chastened in soul by being made a professor. The tourists kept chattering like starlings about the most trivial affairs amid the most sublime scenes, until we betook ourselves to the stillness of the glaciers and the eternal snows.

You will lose all the blessings of the road if you have not the gift of silence. To pass through a wood without snapping a twig. To sit quite still at the foot of a pine tree and let a squirrel come down the trunk and look right into your eyes, wondering if you are a branch. To listen at hot noontide to the breathing of nature as she swoons in her summer sleep. To watch the coming of the dawn from a motionless boat in a Highland loch as the light comes sweeping up behind the eastern hills and the new day is ushered in with a sigh of winds and the twittering of awaking birds.

All this is only possible to a man of silence. Therefore, be still and thou shalt know.

The Ninth Commandment is—THOU SHALT BLAZE THY TRAIL WITH GOOD DEEDS.

Some one is sure to ask if you have passed this way. If so, may the question bring a word of good commendation from every cottage door, and a smile to the faces of the children in every village. Let every tramper behave so on the road that he will receive a welcome when he passes that way again. I have known a wandering man to leave the trail of the serpent behind him in Highland glens and on Hebrid Isles. Not for him the welcome back. So if you would travel the old roads again see that you walk worthily. Here is a legend for all true trampers : " I shall pass through this world but once : any good, therefore, I can do or any kindness that I can show, to any human being, let me do it now, let me not defer it, or neglect it, for I shall not pass this way again."

The Tenth Commandment is — SECURE GOOD LODGMENT FOR THE NIGHT, AND THY SLEEP SHALL BE SWEET.

The end of the longest road comes at last. With weariness, but without fatigue, the wandering man arrives at the wayside inn, hungry with health, and ready to rest. How delicious it is to " change the feet," as we say, and enjoy the evening meal, when the sun goes down behind the hills or over the tranquil sea. The last whaup is crying on the moor before it departs, and the white birds are wailing on the edge of the tide. A whiff of peat reek scents the evening air. Then, the stillness of the summer night, clean sheets, and a sound, dreamless sleep. These are the joys of the road which gold can never buy, but which are open to every wayfaring man who keeps the commandments.

THE ROAD TO THE ISLES
POETRY, LORE, AND TRADITION
OF THE HEBRIDES

By KENNETH MACLEOD

With an Introduction by MARJORY KENNEDY-FRASER
With Map End-paper and Decorations

Price **7s. 6d.,** *postage* **5d.**

THE BEAUTIFUL ISLE OF MULL
WITH IONA AND THE ISLE OF SAINTS

By THOMAS HANNAN

With 16 Illustrations from Photographs by the Author
and Map End-paper

Price **7s. 6d.,** *postage* **4d.**

By the VERY REV. CHARLES L. WARR, St Giles Cathedral

THE UNSEEN HOST
STORIES OF THE GREAT WAR

New and Enlarged Edition   *Price* **5s.,** *postage* **4d.**

THE CALL OF THE ISLAND
FIVE TALES

Containing The Call of the Island; The Christ of the Trenches;
The Death Music; The Lady of Laggan; St Bride of the Mantle

Price **7s. 6d.,** *postage* **6d.**

ROBERT GRANT & SON
126 PRINCES STREET, EDINBURGH

Demy Octavo, 224 *pages*, 20 *Plates*, *Full Cloth*, *Gilt*
10s. 6d. *net*; *post free* 11s.

THE SEVEN AGES OF AN EAST LOTHIAN PARISH BEING THE STORY OF WHITTINGEHAME FROM EARLIEST TIMES

BY

MARSHALL B. LANG, T.D., B.D.
Minister of Whittingehame

WITH FOREWORD BY
'THE LADY FRANCES BALFOUR

CONTENTS

Pre-Historic—The Dawn of History—
Early Christian Period—Mediæval Period
—Reformation Period—Seventeenth and
Eighteenth Centuries—Modern—Families
of Whittingehame — Place Names of
the Parish

ROBERT GRANT & SON
126 PRINCES STREET, EDINBURGH

"Is e deireadh nan Gàidheal a bhi falamh

The Outer Hebrides

Lewis

Bull of Lewis

Stornoway

The Minch

Harris

North Uist

Kunish Head

Trotternish

Ewe

Gairloch

Vaternish

Durnish

Isle

of

SKYE

Portree

The Little Minch

South Uist

Kintail

Sleat

Barra